AF442295

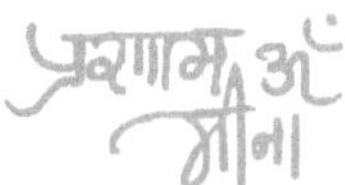

प्रणाम अँ
मीना

NITYA GEETA

Anaadi Satya – Eternal Truth

PRANAM
Meena Om

Pranam Prakshan

While the human mind backed with ego of conquering the world, goes on running here and there creating all types of scientific gadgets and collecting knowledge for manipulating things or winning nature, Nature silently prepares a medium to show the human ego how small it is. Nature silently, effortlessly, with her own tests and measuring scales of intelligence, evolves a species that is totally of her mind, according to Nature's free will. Free will that is not under the influence of any insisting, designing or forcing... It goes on creating, discarding imperfection simultaneously, to make the 'chosen one' surface at the right time according to time requirement, knowing fully well that the outcome will be just beautiful.

|| ॐ ||

The truth is here.
Let us join hands to be part of the Pranam Movement
✻ To awaken India to its true spiritual potential
✻ To merge Ved and Vigyan, Vidya and Gyan
✻ To experience the joy of being a real
human being

|| ॐ ||

Pranam
Gratitude
Love
And Salutations
To All
Who have firmly resolved to
transform absolutely and are dedicated to
Mana Marg — the infallible path of Pranam
based on Truth Love Karm and Light.

PRANAM is a movement to spread Truth Love Karm and
Light for spiritual blossoming, to realise the joy of being a
real human being, the perfect creation of Nature. Our goal is
transformation, whole and complete — spiritual social political
and economic — based on the guidance of
the eternal truth of Nature's Law.

Translation: Anubhuti
Editing: Manasvini
Design: Jaspal S Bisht
Published by Pranam Prakashan, Noida
www.pranam.org.in
pranam@divinedesign.in
First Print Edition - 2024

Copyright © Meena Om 2024
All Rights Reserved.

ISBN 979-8-89446-017-8

Contents

ॐ

Preface

Humble Supplication
Vinamra Nivedan

Om Shreemad Bhagwad Geeta has an unparalleled superb stature in world literature. This is a divine supreme mystic speech that directly emanated from the mouth of the manifested Prabhu. In the Geeta, the Prabhu himself through the medium of Arjun imparts a sermon for the welfare of humanity. In this small scripture, Prabhu has revealed those unknown and remarkable feels of his heart which none could fathom whole and complete till now.

I am immensely gratified that due to the grace of Prabhu Shree Pyare ji — Shree Krishn, I got this five-elemental body temple of the lineage of the family devoted to Maa Saraswati.

In adolescence, my being got the opportunity to read a commentary on the Geeta by Acharya ji, an elder cousin brother. Being young I could not understand it fully but the curiosity to learn more about it got awakened. When by the benevolence of my dear Prabhu, I did yatra of Bharat bare foot, a copy of the Geeta Dainandini — Geeta journal — by Geeta Press was my companion. While resting in the

shadow of trees in the afternoons, I studied the Geeta. It imparted intense peace, even fatigue vanished. Within nine months I lost count of how many times I read it, but every time I got new insights out of it. When I started living at the ashram, then I got the chance to read, understand the commentaries of many great scholars and various other famous Geetas, such as Ashtavakra Geeta and others.

Today by the infinite grace of Shree Pyare ji, I got the opportunity to go through and understand the Nitya Geeta by 'Manu' — Pranam Meena Om. This is due to the blessings of my revered parents and Param Pujya Guru ji. Respected Meena ji has delved deep into the deepest, profound ocean of the Geeta and found and brought to light numerous secret precious jewels. These have been scripted in a very simple and concise manner with her generosity for the welfare of sadhaks. In my opinion, this 'descended gyan' in the form of Nitya Geeta is very different, wonderful splendid and exceptional than commentaries on the Geeta. Its name itself reveals many divine feels and meanings. To indicate dialogues of Krishn and Arjun the symbol of sudarshan chakra and arrow have made it very attractive.

The Shree Krishn Bhupoor Yantra given at the end is absolutely marvellous; maybe it is the new message

and best gift for this Yug. Though I am being asked to define and explain it, however, I feel that one has to reach a certain level of consciousness to be able to convey the truth about it, or may be even a higher level, to define the tattve, the essence of this yantra. Then that explanation may take the form of a fabulous scripture.

The Nitya Geeta has not been written or scripted in accordance with some philosophical point of view or to display scholarly skills and wisdom but with one purpose — welfare of all. The Nitya Geeta is beneficial to every sadhak of any caste creed sect language or country who wants to have absolute peace.

I humbly request all the loved ones of Shree Krishn Pyare ji to read, study and understand this pearl of wisdom with full concentration because no one else could have presented it in such a simple language. To derive maximum benefit out of it, endeavour to imbibe it as much as possible in your conduct.

Hariom Tatt Satt

Shrotriye Brahmnisht Shree 108
Swami Mangal Teerth ji Maharaj 'Gopadrenu'
Kasaragod, Kerala

Melody of Geeta
Sugeeta

Krishn's flute plays
Like a bugle of peace
Like meena's heart
Like a statement of truth
Like a dream of love
Like the life-breath of Radha
Like an expansion of karm
Like an awakening call
Like a new dawn of life
Like laws of the Veds
Like the soulmate of Krishn
meena neither sleeps nor is awake
Like the pupil of the eye of the Universe
Like the chosen one
Smiling within...
Like Durga, the Brahmvaadini meena*
The Self-realised meena manu...

This is Truth
Truth is here.

** Brahmvaadini – the spokesperson of Supreme*

|| ॐ ||

Introduction

Param Anubhuti — Supreme Realisation Through Sentience

> The story
> Starts with me
> And ends at me.
> Then again,
> It starts with me
> New, afresh
> In a new Avtar.

These words are not philosophy. It is possible for each one of us to realise our true potential and blossom fully. The Nitya Geeta is the outcome of divine blessings that were bestowed upon my humble being. Life has been a constant sadhna of trying to know what lies beyond the worldly mire. Through a series of realisations, this version of the Geeta started to manifest, bit by bit, through frequent trance writings.

My connection with Shree Krishn is that of non-duality. To attain Brahmpad, the supreme state of Being, is to be absolutely anchored in Krishn Consciousness, which is entrenched in Supreme Reality. To feel this Supreme Reality and the pedestal of Krishn is unlike anything in this world. It is the essence of satyam shivam sunderam – truthful, welfare

of all, beautiful. After experiencing it, the entire world appears to be dull, insipid and meaningless.

Floating in Brahmand, that infinite space, there is no sense of Time, Age, or gait. Colours are pure and different from those seen here, neither too dense nor too light. It feels like one knows the secret of the whole Universe and all Ages. Nothing remains to be known. Everything is so unlike what we see, feel and say here. There is no blinking of an eyelid, just an awareness of being a spark of that whole and complete — Poornta. As soon as the feeling of knowing something emerges, it manifests into reality. One can observe and feel any time-period in totality.

Floating like a ball of cotton, up-down, here-there, everywhere. In one second beholding the beginning of Creation, in another, seeing Kaliyug, the age of machines, unfolding. Leaping from one timespan to another without feeling the distance. Only being conscious of the space. Everything is whole, complete and encapsulated. The feeling is of knowing everything and belonging to everyone and yet being a mere witness. There are no relations — no mother father brother sister — no society, not even the feel of the mind, body or self.

The need to ask questions to know answers does not arise. The minute some curiosity arises within, the answer manifests. One is steeped in absolute grace and an all-encompassing 'wholistic' beauty. Words cannot

explain it; they become powerless and meaningless. Even worldly sciences cannot describe this ultimate bliss. To express the beauty of this experience, only a feeble attempt can be made through eyes, speech and gestures. Perhaps those who have experienced transcendental state can relate to this grace and comprehend it in some manner. Can the taste of taste be described without tasting; can one grasp the shape of clouds without seeing or describe the perfect colours and form of the rainbow without witnessing.... Even after tasting, feeling and seeing, these are difficult to express. They can only be experienced.

As the Nitya Geeta descended, some bhavs, feels, also manifested in the worldly domain. The image of Shree Krishn on the first page was a humble attempt to capture his grace and beauty as witnessed in my deep trance. The various conch shells drawn within the manuscript are also outcomes of dhyan.

Contrary to worldly syntax, question marks are not used anywhere in the text, because the Universe has no questions. In some places, there are no commas either, as they tend to alter the flow...

Besides these, my comprehensions are documented and denoted in italics or with a shakti symbol when mentioned within the divine discourse. The select poems and text prior to Chapter One are those that poured in as my being was getting prepared to receive this transcendental, transformative gyan.

Subsequently, the 'Insights into the Geeta' in the second half of the text, are my musings related to this ultimate dialogue between Supreme Intelligence and an inquiring being, a true seeker.

The Nitya Geeta is an effort to reveal the Truth of the highest evolved human Shri Krishn of Dwapar Yug. My astral visits made me realise that if a human follows the mechanism of the Universe, lives according to the laws of Nature and gets connected to Supreme Intelligence, SI, through Yog and Dhyan, as stated by Shri Krishn in the Geeta, one can become the medium to spread Love and Light, to create a world full of peace and bliss.

Kaliyug is the time for absolute amalgamation of Ved and Vigyan, truth and facts; para-apara, worldly and beyond the mind sciences. This can happen only by feeling and realising THAT Param Tattve, Supreme Essence. Let us all aspire to create a better world by being in sync with Nature and our nature.

May we all be open and willing to transform, grow and evolve towards the next step of evolution. By imbibing and living the words of evolved souls, transformation can happen. This is the call of Time.

Pranam
Meena Om

Salutations to the Supreme
Om Shree Parmatmaney Namah

*If this secret knowledge is imparted even
to a dried tree stub, on it too will grow branches
and tender leaves.
In life, the karmkshetra, field of karm becomes
dharmkshetra, field of dharm
Then Krishn Consciousness becomes the Charioteer
and according to time requirement, for the
establishment of the true eternal Sanatan Dharm,
imparts gyan wisdom and directions.*

|| ॐ ||

*In absolute surrender, with humility and gratitude,
may the study and contemplation and reflection of
this essence-filled Nitya Geeta be carried forth by the
grace of Shree Krishn Jagadguru Consciousness.
May human life justify its existence and attain
poornta, become whole and complete
May this be the prayer.*

*Shree Krishnam Vande Jagadgurum
Salutations to Shree Krishn Jagadguru
The guru of the world.*

|| ॐ ||

卐 ॐ 卐
卐

Be Absolutely Blissful
Sachchidanand Ghan Bhav

Be poorn sachchidanand, in absolute
bliss of the truthful soul.

One manifestation has sprouted
Blossomed on Earth as Nature desired
Realised and called herself
The psychic daughter of Nature
Whose aura transforms
The existing forms of worldly actions and conducts...

She is here in the dark night of ignorance
To illumine the lamp of truth
To establish the truth of
The greatest and supreme laws of Nature.

|| 卐 ||

Shree Krishn
The Universal Consciousness

The consciousness that is ever prevalent
Has been given cognisance in the name Krishn
All attractive
All beautiful
Forever truthful
Present in every molecule...

Krishn is the name of Universal Consciousness
All pervading omnipotent and omniscient
Supreme Intellect
Supreme Consciousness...

The state of being Krishn
Is the highest most evolved state
Of human perfection.

|| ॐ ||

Journey of Life

To become from human to God
From nar to Narayan — male to sublime man
From nari to Narayani — female to sublime woman
To become Jagadeeshwar—
the Master of Creation full of divine qualities
To become Jagadeeshwari —
the reigning force of Creation full of divinity
To become an anukriti of Prakriti —
reflection of Nature
To reveal secrets of the Universe
To emerge from all doubts of birth and death...

To just BE — to live and to flow
To BE and not to BE
Not to BE and yet to BE
For the happening of the unforeseen
To manifest the dream of Creation
To become from a sadhak, practitioner
to prasarak, disseminator
And then vidhayak, spokesperson of Supreme
To become whole and complete
and then to merge with the Absolute.

|| ॐ ||

The Pace and Culmination
of Perfection

I am the consciousness of time and age
In meena form
Poorn, whole and complete
In meena form
Created by Creation
The resonance of creativity
Pranav in meena form
Praman, proof of Supreme Consciousness
In meena form
Pratyaksh, visible manifestation
An evidence in meena form
My expansion is happening with all humility
Pranam in meena form...
I am Ved Vigyan, truth and fact
I am the union of truth and science
I am the song of the soul of the whole Creation
I am signature of Shree Krishn
On the book of Time
This is Truth.

|| 卐 ||

Auspicious Invocation

Om Gurur Brahma Gurur Vishnu
Gurur Devo Maheshwara
Gurur Sakshat Param Brahm
Tasmai Shree Guruvey Namah

Know the Guru to be Brahma himself. He is Vishnu.
He is Shiv. Know Him to be the Supreme Brahm.
Offer thy adorations unto that peerless Guru.

From birth after birth
Since the beginning of Creation
I was
I am
And I will be
From yug to yug
From birth to birth
My gurus are Brahma Vishnu Mahesh themselves.
This is the truth of my being.
This is Truth
Truth is here.

Nitya Geeta

Gayatri Mantra

Om Bhur Bhuvah Swaha
Tat Savitur Vareyniyam
Bhargo Devasya Dheemahi
Dhiyo Yonah Prachodayat

O Supreme, thou art the Giver of life
The Remover of pain and sorrow
The Bestower of happiness
O Creator of the Universe
May we receive Thy supreme sin-destroying light
May Thou guide and inspire
our intellect in the right direction.

O Maa Saraswati

Hail O Mother Saraswati
Salutations to the wielder of the veena
Hail O Lotus-seated Mother
Salutations to the giver of auspicious boons
O Mother, deliver the world
For thou art the destroyer of all obstacles
Hail the one seated on a lotus
Leave your lotus seat
Look at the state of the world
Let flow the river of peace
O Mother, once again in the world...
Salutations to Mother Saraswati
Goddess, we humbly bow to thee
O Sharde, bestow upon us your boon.

Om Saraswatyey Vidhmahe Brahmputrye
Dhimahee Tanno Devi Prachodyat

Om...let me meditate on Goddess Saraswati
O Daughter of Brahma
Give us the intellect
Impart the memory, knowledge and the power
of speech to spread light.

|| ॐ ||

Om Parmatmaney Namah
Shree Krishnam Vande Jagadgurum
Jai Yogeshwar

Wednesday, 4.11.1992   Time: Night 03.20
Om Bram Breem Brom Seh Buddhaye Namah

Chapter 1

Descent of the Geeta
War is Declared — Depression of Arjun

- ☀ Symbol of Shri Krishn
- ➤ Symbol of Arjun
- ✳ Symbol of my realisations

Maharishi Ved Vyas addresses Dhritrashtra: The Great War and massive annihilation of Kshatriyas is inevitable, so imparting divya drishti, divine sight, I enable you to witness the war.

Dhritrashtra declines to witness the destruction of his lineage. Hence, Sanjay is bestowed with the divine vision to know the details of the war and the mental state of its warriors.

Dhritrashtra enquires about the details of the war from Sanjay...

Dhritrashtra: What is transpiring between my sons and the sons of Pandu as they assemble with a desire for war...

Sanjay: Duryodhan is asking Dronacharya to take a look at the war formation and the Pandav army positioned by Dhrishtadyumn, son of Dhrupad.

Dhritrashtra: Who all are in the Pandav army...

Sanjay: Yuyudhan Satyaki Virat Dhrupad Dhrishtaketu Shriaj of Chekitan Kuntibhoj Shaivya Yudhamanyu Uttamauja Abhimanyu and the five sons of Draupadi.

Dhritrashtra: Who are the warriors in the Kaurav army...

Sanjay: Dronacharya Bheeshm Karan Kripacharya Ashwathama Vikaran Bhurishrava and many powerful warriors.

Dhritrashtra: What is Duryodhan thinking after seeing the leaders of both the armies...

Sanjay: His thought is — on my side people like Bheeshm Drona are ubhay pakshpaati, with divided loyalties, while the Pandav army has nij pakshpaati, hence victory will be theirs alone.

✳ *It is true gyan:*
  * *Even if there are just a few nij pakshpaati, there is kalyan, welfare*
  * *Even if there is a high number of ubhay pakshpaati, there is no welfare*
  * *Ubhay pakshpaati, double-minded people, perpetually in duality*
  * *Nij pakshpaati, those who are focused on one side, having one-point programme. Loyalty wins.*

So trying to appease Bheeshm and ensure his loyalty, Duryodhan is asking all his warriors to protect him. Hearing which Bheeshm is blowing his conch that is sounding like a lion's roar. Assuming that the war has begun, all the Kauravs too are blowing their war trumpets together creating a cacophony of fearsome sound.

Then seated on a great chariot drawn by white horses, Shree Krishn blows his conch, the Panchjanya; Arjun with full vigour, his conch the Devdutt; Bhim the Paundra; Yudhishthir the Anant-vijay; Nakul the Sughosh and Sahdev the Manipushpak; all blowing them simultaneously.

This shankh-naad, sound of conches is piercing through the hearts of the unjust Kauravs.

After which Arjun picking up the Gandiv, his bow, is requesting Shree Krishn, the knower of all and the infallible one, to drive his chariot to the centre of the battlefield in between both the armies.

Shree Krishn fulfils the wish of Arjun the nidrajayee, the one who has conquered sleep, to see everyone at a glance.

Seeing all the clans, Arjun is depressed.

»➤ The body is incapacitated and my Gandiv is slipping. I can see inauspicious omens and no benefit in killing family members.

☀ How to get the throne without killing them...

»➤ O Krishn, I do not want victory or kingdom, nor do I want happiness, O Govind, what is to be gained by such a kingdom, such luxuries or even such a life...

☀ Why don't you want victory...

»➤ Our clan-members for whom we want all the luxuries and happiness are assembled here for war...

✴ And if they kill you, then...

»➤ Will not kill them even for the kingdom comprising all the three worlds. This is only the Earth!

✴ Why don't you want the joy of winning the kingdom...

»➤ What happiness or pleasure is there in killing relatives...

✴ Why are they ready to kill then...

»➤ They have lost their wisdom due to greed. They cannot fathom the fallout of the war — the destruction of the clan and the resultant ill-will.

✴ What will happen if the clan is destroyed...

»➤ The dharm of our clan, prevalent kul-dharm will be destroyed; adharm will become rampant and with this, lawlessness will prevail; women will get sullied, leading to the birth of mixed breeds who cannot be the cause of the deliverance of ancestors through rituals like shraadh and tarpan. The clan becomes hell bound by the destruction of dharm of caste and creed.

If you knew the repercussions of war, why did you agree to it...

This great sin has been committed; that is why they are ready to destroy kith and kin... I am renouncing the war, it is better to die.

Thus abandoning his bow, Arjun sits down in the middle of the chariot.

|| ॐ ||

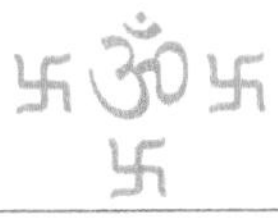

Om Parmatmaney Namah

Shree Krishnam Vande Jagadgurum

Jai Yogeshwar

Wednesday, 11.11.1992   Time: Night 11.40

Om Bram Breem Brom Seh Buddhaye Namah

Chapter 2

Karm Dharm Gyan Yog

Dhritrashtra: What is the condition of Arjun seated in the centre of the chariot...

Sanjay: Teary-eyed, depressed and overpowered by cowardice.

- Cowardice is not a worthy adornment of a noble man. Neither does it assist in attaining heaven, nor does it provide glory. Forego weakness of the heart and fight.

- I am not scared of dying but of killing. Even sharp rude words ought not to be uttered to the revered ones, how to shower arrows at them...

- Does one see something else while performing one's duty...

»➤ Sweets are good but what is the value of such bhog, luxuries after slaughtering one's gurus... Is it right to kill those standing in front, after killing whom one does not even want to live...

☀ In this state of indecision what have you thought Arjun... What solution have you thought of...

»➤ Cowardice has covered my Kshatriye dharm and the mind is incapable of taking a decision that adheres to the dharm... O Prabhu! Impart to me guidance and wisdom.

Dhritrashtra: Then what happened...

Sanjay: I do not want to fight, I will not fight, states Arjun clearly, puts the Gandiv down and becomes silent.

☀ You mourn for those who are not worthy of being mourned. Wise ones, pandits do not mourn for both, the alive and the dead.

»➤ Why...

☀ We, you and I and all the kings, have existed earlier also, are here today and will be there in the future too, so why grieve; as the body goes through the stages of adolescence youth and old age, the wise ones are not under any illusion regarding these. All the subjects of the senses impart happiness or pain according to their favourable and unfavourable states. Everything that comes and goes is anitya, impermanent.

So Arjun, stay flawless.

Be equipoised in sukh, happiness, and dukh, sorrow.

The one who is not attached to either happiness or sorrow attains the Paramatma, the Supreme Soul, through a swataha-siddh amarta, self-realised immortality.

✴ *I know this as Truth.*
The word 'Truth' written at 12.10 midnight.

❋ The reign of Truth — the element of consciousness is unchangeable.

The unreal has no permanent existence. The real never ceases to be. Knowing the gyan, tattve gyan of both, the tattve-darshi, seers who know the essence, attain immortality.

- Truth is indestructible and pervades the entire world. No one can destroy it
- Falsehood is perishable; it is bound to be destroyed. So do your duty, O Arjun!
- The eternal immortal essence — the soul, neither dies nor is annihilated

- It is nitya, eternal; nirantar, constant; shashwat, perpetual; and anaadi, having neither a beginning nor an end — that which has existed since eternity and does not die even when the body is killed
- Only the body dies, the imperishable soul casts off the old shell to take up a new one, just like discarding old clothes and adorning the new
- The soul cannot be cut with worldly weapons
  Air cannot dry it
  Fire cannot burn it
  Water cannot wet it because it is constantly there in all, poorn, whole and complete unaffected eternal and established in its consistent truth. It cannot be seen in a form.
- Do not grieve for the physical body because whosoever is born is sure to die. The one who has died is sure to be reborn. This is Nature's law. So do not grieve.
  Aprakat, unmanifest after death
  Aprakat before birth
  It manifests only in the middle, so why grieve.

»➤ What is the cause of grief, O Prabho...

☀ Ignorance, not knowing. The experience of this realisation happens on its own. The one who resides in the physical frame cannot be killed, is consistent and eternal.

So do not grieve.

»➤ You have stated the remedy to get rid of grief but how to get rid of the fear of sin...

✴ Kshatriye dharm — for a warrior there is no greater redeeming karm than fighting for dharm.

»➤ Should a kshatriya, warrior, continue to fight wars...

✴ No, the war that befalls upon you on its own is the path to heaven. Real anand is devoid of happiness and sorrow. The attainment of bhog, enjoyments or indulgence, is not the cause of great happiness but of sorrow instead.

»➤ What if I do not fight the war that has come on its own...

✴ The glory of the kshatriye dharm will be tarnished and you will be committing the sin of not performing your duty.

»➤ What is the result of disgrace.

✴ It will be a subject of discussion far and wide; for honourable men defamation is even more painful than death. You will become insignificant in the eyes of the high and noble men like Bheeshm and Drona. Known as someone who ran away from war because of the fear of dying, you will be criticised. What could be more painful than this... If you get killed in the war you shall go to heaven, on winning, rule the Earth. So stand up and decide to fight. Fight this war by maintaining sambuddhi, equanimity in victory-defeat, gain-loss, happiness-sorrow; there is no sin in this.

»➤ Dear Prabho, how to maintain equanimity...

☀ Now listen to its greatness in karm yog:

- The one who has equanimity is freed from all karm bandhan, ties of karm
- Equanimity is never depleted
- There is no contradictory effect of this anushthan, exercise; sadhna, practise
- Even the faintest association with this practice protects one from the great fear of birth and death.

»➤ What is the way to attain sambuddhi, O Prabho...

☀ The mind that has a one-point programme to realise the Paramatma is always balanced...

The ones who do not have this single-minded resolve to realise the Paramatma have minds that have unending and multipronged, numerous branches.

»➤ What are the signs of a multipronged mind...

❋ Engrossed in desires

- Always assuming heaven to be shreshth, best
- Passionate about result-oriented deeds as stated in the Veds, shastras
- Having no other focus than bhog
- Such an ignorant human uses showy flowery speech that propels him towards bearing the fruits of his karma collected since birth; that speech is very descriptive of the various deeds performed in pursuit of bhog and worldly opulence.

»➤ Can those with a distracted mind have a one-point programme or not...

❋ A mind attracted to bhog, humans with a sense of attachment, cannot have a one-point programme to attain the Divine. It just cannot be!

»➤ What is the way to overcome attachments...

❋ The Veds explain the three gunas, attributes, and their worldly functions. So O Arjun, be detached from the sakaam karm, attachment causing deeds mentioned in the Veds.

- Be devoid of indulgence jealousy and conflicts
- Be fixed in the eternal endless Paramatm Tattve, Supreme Essence
- Be free from the worry of protecting that which you have and to gain that which you have not
- Be completely dedicated to that Supreme Paramatma
- Have only one aim, to attain the Divine.

➤ By doing this, what kind of state will it be...

❋ Just as upon reaching a big lake, smaller ponds lose significance, similarly in the eyes of the liberated tattvagya, the one who knows the meaning and significance of the Ved, shastras, the world and its bhog become insignificant.

➤ O Prabho, is there a way for me to achieve this state...

❋ Yes, through karm yog, doing deeds without the desire for results. Do not be attached — even to the body mind and sense organs that perform karm.

»➤ Then why perform any karm at all...

❋ There should never be any inclination for not doing karm.

»➤ How to do karm...

❋ Yog is being same in siddhi and asiddhi, accomplishment and non-accomplishment.

Renounce attachment and perform karm firmly established in equanimity... constant karm... consistent karm.

»➤ If I perform karm without yog and equanimity, then...

❋ Without equanimity, karm with the desire for results is of the lowest grade. Take refuge in sambuddhi, equanimity, O Dhananjay. Those who are working for results are narrow-minded, slaves of results.

»➤ Who is better...

❋ The human who has sambuddhi is best...

- He is without paap-punya , sin and virtue while alive; so be firmly established in equanimity
- Equanimity in karm is proficiency

- Manishis, the wise ones renounce the fruit of their karm to become free from the bondage of birth and attain the nirvikar state, the state of supreme flawlessness.

»➤ How to know that allurement of the fruit of karm has been renounced...

☀ When the buddhi, intellect, sails unaffected through the marshes of attachment, it becomes indifferent towards the bhog that one is going through or will go through.

»➤ After being dispassionate, when does one attain equanimity...

☀ When a mind disillusioned by worldly principles and contradictory opinions gets detached from these, turns towards the Paramatma and remains firm in it, attains equanimity — that is the result of yog sadhna.

»➤ What are the indications of a balanced buddhi that has attained equanimity...

☀ Renouncing all desires, being content in itself, absolutely centred within the self, such a person is called sthitpragya.

»➤ How does a sthitpragya speak and conduct himself...

☀ His speech and conduct are not according to normal action-reaction but based on bhav, feel.

- Emotionally undisturbed when faced with dukh, sorrow
- Nor elated when experiencing sukh, happiness
- Free from obsession fear and anger, with a constantly manansheel, contemplative mind
- Be sthitpragya, stable minded; have sthirbuddhi.

✳ *Have to attain Paramatma. That has been established now.*

☀ A sthitpragya sits like a tortoise contracting all his senses.

»➤ How to identify the one whose senses have contracted...

☀ Dispassion happens when senses are removed from the subjects of senses. But renouncement of ras bhog, taste of tastes; sukh bhog, constant thought of satisfaction of desires, happens only to a sthitpragya human who is realised or enlightened.

- As long as there is ras buddhi, mind that is indulgent in ras bhog, even the wisest one who is in sadhna can become enslaved.

➤ How to remove ras buddhi...

☀ Control all your senses and direct them towards the Divine.

- Not being absorbed in the Divine, you will be mentally preoccupied with various subjects and be allured by them
- From allurement arises desire, if desire is not fulfilled there arises anger, from anger emerges sammoh, obsession, from obsession comes moodhta, idiocity
- By idiocity smriti, memory, is destroyed and by the destruction of smriti, all the satt sankalps, truthful resolves of the sadhak, fade into oblivion
- When memory is destroyed, vivek buddhi, the intellect that differentiates between right and wrong, gets annihilated
- Due to suppression of the power of wisdom and destruction of the intellect, the human faces ruination
- A sthitpragya, devoid of raag-dvesh, hate and resentment, attains the joy within
- All sorrows are destroyed and the buddhi of a sthitpragya is firmly established in Supreme.

»➤ Who is the one whose buddhi is not firm...

☀ The one whose mind and senses are not controlled or disciplined...

- The one who does not have an ek nischaya wali buddhi, intellect with a single-minded resolve
- Does not think of fulfilling his duties, is ashaant, restless.

»➤ There is no possibility of the mind of a bhogi being firm but why not that of a sadhak...

☀ Just like a boat floating on water is carried away by the wind, in the same way, the mann, heart-mind, is led astray by the senses; the one who leaves vishaya chintan, who ceases to think about subjects, he is a true sthitpragya.

- Common men have no control over their senses, they are asleep with regard to attaining the Divine; it is night for them
- The one whose senses are in control, for such a disciplined person it is always daytime, for he is forever awake
- For a person who has control over the senses, the presence of bhog does not create any vikaar, ripples and vices within

- Only such a person attains absolute peace and the Paramatm-tattve, the Supreme soul essence
- Peace is attained by renouncing bhog. Renounce all desires and spriha, cravings...
- Only the one who is without ahanta-mamta, attachment and possessiveness attains peace Such a person is established in the Brahm...
- This is Braahmi sthiti, the state of being Aham Brahmasmi, 'I am Brahm'
- Once this is attained human never gets allured
- Even at the last moment if this state devoid of ahanta-mamta, mine-thine dawns, the human attains Brahm and nirvaan.

|| ॐ ||

The Chain of Avtars

Aligned with the chain of avtars
Strung in the same garland
From Matasyavtar to Kalki
The journey is my journey

Avtar Consciousness acquires a body
That takes it where it has to reach
From there it shall take another form...

Avtar Consciousness will change bodies
Effortlessly, like changing old clothes
Forever guiding
Giving directives and messages
Witnessing the whole cosmic play
Sampoorn, whole and complete

Do not miss it this time
Because it has been disclosed to you
What is Consciousness...
The state of an avtar and its swaroop, form.

Sadhguru and Avtar

A sadhguru can do a lot, impart knowledge education morals sanskars, annihilate fears, provide peace and direction. He can show humans the path of liberation and enlightenment. But there are two things that only an Avtar can do — one, absolute deliverance and the other, on the call of a true bhakt, devotee, go rushing to him and protect his honour.

Even Bheeshm Pitamah while lying on a bed of arrows remembered not his gurus but Madhusudan, as Shree Krishn was also known. Shree Krishn too disregarded everything and went on his call.

Before the war, Shree Krishn revealed his viraat roop, his supreme vast form, to the entire assembly and yet they were ready to fight against him. They did not acknowledge the living truth present before them, nor did they pay any heed to his advice to refrain from war.

Who touches the feet of an Avtar... either the ones who are younger to him, an ananya, extraordinary, devotee such as Shree Hanuman or a beloved like Shree Radha.

An Avtar performs all his worldly duties and deeds till the very end, whereas for guru-swamis these are bondages. Although in the Treta yug and Dwapar

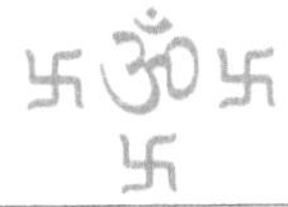

yug, many maharishis, swamis and gurus spent their lives with equally wise life-partners, but by the time of Kali yug, the thought that grihasth, family life, is a burden, an attachment, became prevalent. Run, renounce and protect yourself even from the shadow of a woman!

An Avtar is an example of Truth Love Karm and Light. He manifests for the deliverance of human and humanity.

- *He is sarvkala sampoorn, a master of all arts*
- *Going beyond his own respect, dis-respect, he honours all guru-swamis as deemed fit*
- *He rushes at the call of the bhakt who is in complete surrender*
- *He clears all doubts and dualities of a deserving one in peril*
- *Every word of his is truthful. He is the spokesperson of Supreme Consciousness.*

An Avtar manifests for the deliverance of those beings who are in constant reverence, for example, Ahilya, Kewat, Shabri; runs to the rescue on the call of Draupadi and Gajendra; becomes the charioteer of Arjun. All this can be done only by an Avtar for a bhakt who is in absolute submission and engrossed in him.

An Avtar pays obeisance to all gurus, says pranam and touches their feet. He conducts the dharm of sewa and satkaar, service and reverence, with complete devotion. All gurus know and recognise an Avtari, the manifestation, but who acknowledges! They only know how to get assistance and support of his divine attributes.

In Treta yug, when their yagyas were being disrupted, gurus Vasishth and Vishwamitr took teenagers Ram and Lakshman to fight the demons.

In Dwapar yug, as soon as Shree Krishn stepped into his teens, Akrur came to fetch him to revolt against the atrocities of Kans and to slay him.

Who wants to know the feelings of an Avtar! It is the destiny and dharm of the Avtar to renounce all his desires and aspirations, leave behind thrones and Radhas for the purpose of human welfare and walk on the path of true dharm and duty karm.

All this is beyond the intellect of a common human. The Avtar is sensitive towards the entire Creation but who is sensitive towards him... The one who synchronises the whole Universe, who is in sync with his human form...

The presence of the Avtar gives bliss that is why when he moves away there is virah, pining and separation pangs. They show him plenty of love for their own selfish reasons, to avoid the pain of virah. That the Avtar too might have some emotional needs, this is completely overlooked by all relatives associates friends gurus and swamis. This is the irony and destiny of an Avtar.

This is Truth
Truth is here.

|| ॐ ||

ॐ

Om Parmatmaney Namah
Shree Krishnam Vande Jagadgurum
Jai Yogeshwar

Wednesday, 25.11.1992   Time: Night 1.40

Om Bram Breem Brom Seh Buddhaye Namah

Chapter 3

The Gyan of Duty Karm

➤ If equanimity is the noblest thing then why perform karm.
I am confused, please clarify, O Prabho...

☀ Sankhya yogis swear allegiance to gyan yog. Yogis pledge allegiance to karm yog. Gyan yog + karm yog = attainment of sambuddhi. It is essential to perform karm to attain equanimity. By renouncing karm, siddhi, accomplishment cannot be attained...

- So equanimity cannot be attained without initiating karm or by renouncing karm
- No human can survive without performing karm. It is the natural instinct of human...
- Sitting silently is not renouncing karm, it is mithyachaar, false conduct.

»➤ How to attain sambuddhi, O Prabho...

☀ By restraining the senses even in the mind, devoid of any attachment, performing ones 'duty-karm' nishkaam, without expectations

- Such a person is shreshth, superb; he is equanimous
- A human being gets tied to karm when he works only for himself
- So do karm to perform kartavya karm, duty-karm, and to secure the parampara, tradition of karm.

»➤ Why work when there is no desire for fruits of action...

☀ At the commencement of sarg, the cycle of Creation, Brahma created and stated: Through the yagya of kartavya karm attain buddhi-vriddhi, intellect and growth.

»➤ What should be the yagya bhav, feeling behind the yagya...

☀ May there be rise in the number of humans with divine qualities and attributes...

- May devtas and noble men enhance you

- Performing of duty-karm is paramount
- Equanimity is experienced only by doing duties that are for the welfare of others.

»➤ What is the focus of kartavya karm...

✹ Managing Creation. Even Krishn Consciousness engages in kartavya karm....

- The process of duty-karm is stated in the Veds
- Paramatma, the Supreme soul, dwells in the Veds
- The one who does not work to preserve the sanctity of the cycle of Creation, he lives in vain
- The one who performs karm without attachment is satisfied, content. Such a selfless person is considered a mahapurush, great human
- Supreme is attained through dispassionate karm, for example, King Janak, who even after attaining Paramatma continued karm for Lok Sangreh, the benefit of all; resurrecting goodness, saving the world from undesirable wrongful paths and taking it towards righteousness. Hence, you too must observe your duty-karm.

✻ *The Geeta gyan begins — lok sangreh, collection of resources for the welfare of masses. The duty-karm of bringing the world back from ku-marg, the undesirable path, to san-marg, the righteous path.*

How does lok sangreh happen, O Prabho...

It is done in two ways:

- Through your readiness to do your duty,
- Through the words of shreshth, noble humans and by following them.

King Janak is an example of supreme lok sangreh; is there anyone else who is an example of the same...

I am an example...I have no duty left pending, neither do I have anything left to achieve, yet I do designated karm constantly, consistently for lok sangreh... have to do it...

Why does Prabhu need to work...

To become an example!

What will happen by this...

If I do not do my kartavya karm, everything will get disorganised disturbed and destroyed and I will be the creator of these imperfections, impurities and will have to destroy them too.

Kartavya karm might be essential for you but why for the one who is a tattve gyani, knower of the essence, liberated...

☀ Even for a tattve gyani, to become an example and inspiration for lok sangreh.

➤ What is the difference in performance of karm by a gyani, wise one, and an agyani, ignorant one...

☀ An ignorant person thinks he is the doer.

A gyani remains dispassionate by thinking that all actions are happening in the Brahmswaroop, Nature, a reflection of the Brahm.

➤ Prabho! The amount of responsibility you have, does the tattve gyani also have the same...

☀ He should neither get affected or disturbed by the behaviour of others, ignorant ones, due to attachments, nor should he disturb others... knowing that 'gunn hee gunnon ko barat rahe hain', it is only the gunas that are interacting with each other.

➤ What should I do if disturbed...

☀ Do your duty-karm without santaap, desire and vexation. The battle of life has to be fought with perfection against imperfection. But through the wise intellect, offer all karm to me.

➤ The benefit of offering, Prabho!

❋ Liberation from all ties of karma, cycle of birth and death.

- By not walking this path, life gets denigrated
- A wise person acts according to his nature
- An ignorant person gets entangled in karma due to a mind that is full of raag-dvesh, attachment-resentment and expectations. Such a person has no control over performing karm according to maryada, worldly discipline and right conduct. Hence, denouement is inevitable.

⟫➤ The way to save oneself from this...

❋ Do not perform karm under the influence of raag-dvesh, desires, resentment and competition. While doing ones dharm of duty karm, ones svadharm, own dharm, even if imperfect, is higher and better. Dying while performing ones dharm is the cause of deliverance.

⟫➤ If following dharm is the best, where does the inspiration for adharm, misconduct, come from...

❋ From kaam and kaamna, lust and desires, erupting from rajogunn. These are also the causes of anger.

»➤ What is the work of this mahapaapi kaam, the most sinful — lust...

☀ Just like smoke covers the fire, dust covers the mirror and embryo is covered by the womb, kaam covers the wisdom of a wise sadhak by suppressing the aspiration to not commit a sin. Kaam is an enemy of the wise sadhak. It dwells in the mind, intellect and the senses. 'Doership' covers the knowledge of the one who indulges in deha-abhiman, ego of the self, and eclipses the wisdom.

☀ O Arjun, first of all, control your senses, kill and win over this mahapaapi, great sinner, who stifles all gyan vigyan, wisdom and science...

- The senses are above the body — greater, stronger and enlightened
- The mind is above the senses — greater and vaster
- The intellect is above the mind — greater and more subtle
- Lust is above the intellect — forceful
- Lust lives in the ego and sense of 'doership'. The doer is attracted to objects. Ego also has Nature's jadh, matter aspect, along with a part of the Supreme Essence, Parmeshwar, which

naturally gets attracted to both Nature and Supreme. So, rein yourself in, kill this strong enemy called lust, gain victory over it, O Mahabaho, strong and long-armed one.

|| ॐ ||

Om Parmatmaney Namah
Shree Krishnam Vande Jagadgurum
Jai Yogeshwar

Wednesday, 9.12.1992   Time: Night 12.20
Om Bram Breem Brom Seh Buddhaye Namah

Chapter 4

Divine Knowledge of the Essence
The Eternal Tradition of Karm Yog

Initially, bestowed on the Sun, who passed it on to the progenitor of humanity, Manu, who then bestowed this eternal wisdom to Ikshvaku. Due to the dearth of worthy gurus and a long time lapse, this divine knowledge got lost. The tradition of this constant and consistent sanatan yog vidya that is being shared with you today, got disintegrated with time. It is being imparted to you because you are my friend and devotee...

Gratitude, O Prabho... received through your benevolence this alaukik, ethereal, divine prasad. Where were you at the beginning of Creation, Prabho!

I have taken many births, this is the truth.

You too have taken many births.

I know everything, remember everything, you do not.

I am the Master. I am unborn, imperishable and Master of all beings. Established as their Eeshwar, keeping my nature under control, I manifest through yog maya, my own divine will. Whenever there is decline in dharm and increase in adharm, I manifest as an Avtar.

➤ What is the purpose of the manifestation of an Avtar...

❋ The protection of saints, devotees, annihilation of evil and righteously reinstating dharm. I take birth in every yug.

➤ Why do you not get bound in the karma cycle by repeatedly taking birth...

❋ My birth and my karm are both divine, there's no selfish motive, I manifest only for the welfare of the world. The one who realises me through this tattve gyan attains me.

➤ What is the proof of this...

❋ The ones who are forever absorbed in me...

- Reliant on me, whole and complete, such men and women, by absolute gyan, are able to recognise my karm and birth
- Knowing the divinity of birth and karm through the essence of wisdom, renouncing resentment, fear and anger, attain me
- Taking refuge in me, they too give up selfishness and pride and become eager to work for the welfare of others.

»➤ Then why do people leave you and worship other devi-devtas, gods and goddesses...

☀ They assume and think that the world is more important and want karmjanya siddhi, fruit and accomplishment of their actions.

»➤ Just like devi-devtas and deities are worshipped for karmjanya siddhi, similarly to accomplish some special purpose you too must be performing some deeds ...

☀ According to the karm and qualities of beings, I have divided them into four varnas. But the karm of managing the creation of the universe, I perform without a sense of 'doership', expectation of results.The one who performs karm knowing this essence does not get bound by karm.

»➤ What is karm...

⁕ Remaining unaffected while performing karm, seeing non-action in action. Only that yogi is intelligent who performs karm stoically, whose every action is without any sankalp, resolve. Such a gyani is wise, and forever content.

The one who has control over the body and antahkaran, inner-self; has renounced all kinds of sangrah, accumulation; has no expectations from the world, such a sadhak, although he performs the essential karm related to the body, is not tied by it.

He remains satisfied in every situation; without jealousy and duality; equal in siddhi-asiddhi, accomplishment-non-accomplishment; dispassionate; is forever free and has a single-minded resolve to attain Supreme. A person with such an intellect alone gets all his karm dissolved; becomes akarm, without any karmic reaction. Just a single resolve to attain Supreme is in itself an absolute yagya, constant karm.

»➤ O Prabho! How many types of such yagyas are there...

⁕ Brahm yagya – when all kaaran, cause; upkaran, tools; samagri, ingredients and contents; along with actions become a reflection of Supreme Brahm.

- Bhagwad arpan roop yagya — when all actions objects and rituals become offerings to Param Tattve, Supreme Entity
- Abhinnta roop yagya — in which the sadhak feels oneness with Supreme
- Sanyam roop yagya — the disciplining of all senses
- Vishaya hawan roop yagya — renouncing resentment and attachment, non-indulgence in objects of senses
- Samadhi roop yagya — holding all actions of the breath senses and mann, heart-mind, while the intellect is awake; nirvikalp, fully aware, and nirlipt, absolutely detached
- Dravya yagya — for the purpose of lok sangrah and lokopchaar, to spend money and resources gladly for the welfare and healing of the masses
- Tapoyagya — to bear gladly all difficulties that come on the path of dharm and duty-karm
- Yog yagya — to remain centred in case of achievement or non-achievement of results and siddhi-asiddhi of karm
- Gyan yagya — constant swadhyay, self-study of the Ved-shastra; naam jap, constant remembrance of Prabhu's name; chintan-mannan, contemplation; dhyan, awareness of Supreme
- Pranayam roop yagya — the controlling, regularising and focussing of the prana vayu,

life breath through poorak rechak kumbhak, inhaling exhaling and retaining of breath with complete awareness

- Stambhvriti pranayam roop yagya — through a disciplined diet along with pranayam, to make the life breath centred at its energy centres. All these yagyas are to snap the association with karm

- Knowing the reality of these yagyas, all the sins of the one who conducts them are washed off

- When sins are annihilated, nectar-like Supreme is attained, Paramatma, Supreme Soul is realised

- For the one who does not perform any of these yagyas, for him even this human plane is not beneficial, forget the other-worldly planes

- All yagyas are karmjanya, performed according to karm

- Gyan yagya is the best because through it all karm and subjects come to an end. Thirty-three koti, kinds of devi-devtas, energy sources are attained.

➤ How to attain gyan...

☀ By being in the company of a quintessence gyani, tattve darshi guru and serving him, he himself will impart true gyan...

- With the attainment of gyan, no moha, enchantment will remain, instead there will be anubhuti, realisation that the Paramatma Tattve — Supreme Element is everywhere...

- Riding the boat of wisdom, even the greatest sinner will cross over, attaining deliverance. Wisdom akin to fire burns all sins
- In this manushya lok, human plane, nothing is as pure as gyan
- The one who has perfected gyan yog through karm yog, direct experience, he certainly attains godhood within himself; realises the Supreme within himself; the state of being Swaymbhu Prabhu, Self-germinating Supreme; Aham Brahmasmi, I am Brahm.

»➤ Prabho! How to attain this wisdom...

The sadhak who has control over his senses, is saadhan paraayan, ready to do sadhna, and faithful, attains this gyan. The one who does not know himself nor does he have any faith in others, such a doubt-ridden human is headed towards disaster.

»➤ How to get rid of doubts...

By being established in equanimity...

- Those who have annihilated all doubts with the true gyan of the essence of karm are not bound by the karm.

By the sword of gyan, cut all doubts that sprout due to ignorance; be established in equanimity; stand up and fulfil your duty of fighting the war.

|| ॐ ||

❋ My Genesis

The fruits of karm earned will have to be endured.
Shree Krishn is the complete human; the knower and 16 kala sampoorn, master of sixteen art forms and the subtlest secrets of all aspects of the essence of gyan-vigyan... to such a bhagwan Shree Krishn, my shat shat naman – hundreds and hundreds of humble salutations...
Simplified and straightened my path...
Immeasurable gratitude, O Prabho!
You have made my diminutive intellect capable of understanding your vidhaan, testament.
Else, how would have I gained gyan...
There is no yog greater than swadhyay yog, self-learning.
To turn from the outer world and look within is the first step towards attaining enlightenment.

|| ꯥ ||

Om Parmatmaney Namah
Shree Krishnam Vande Jagadgurum
Jai Yogeshwar

Wednesday, 16.12.1992   Time: Night 1.45
Om Bram Breem Brom Seh Buddhaye Namah

Chapter 5

Divine Yog of Detachment

➤ Between karm yog and sankhya yog, which one is more kalyankari, welfare oriented...

☀ Both have their own significance but karm yog is considered superior to sankhya yog.

➤ Why is karm yog superior...

☀ A karm yogi bereft of resentment and jealousy is a sanyasi; when without dualities, he becomes free from worldly ties. Results of both karm yog and sankhya yog are the same.

➤ If the fruit is the same then why is one superior to the other...

☀ Without karm yog — that is without having equanimity in siddhi-asiddhi, it is difficult to perfect sankhya yog.

- Sankhya yog — to be established in samroop, true being, seeing the reflection of the Divine in all. A manansheel, contemplative karm yogi soon attains samroop Brahm
- Karm yog — being equanimous through siddhi-asiddhi; winning over the senses; having a pure conscience. A karm yogi who sees himself in all, is not indulgent even while performing karm. This is realising Prabhu, Supreme Tattve.

It is impossible to perfect sankhya yog unless one is firm and equanimous through accomplishment-non-accomplishment.

➤ How does a sankhya yogi remain unaffected from karm...

The sankhya yogi knowing the reality of truth and falsehood remains fixed in truth. He is constantly aware that it is the senses which are at play at all times, using themselves...even while seeing listening touching eating smelling, awake-asleep, breathing-excreting, opening or closing eyes, 'I am not doing anything myself', realising this he remains unaffected.

➤ What is the other way to remain non-indulgent ...Bhagwan

☀ Bhakti yog — unaffected like a lotus in water.

A karm yogi is dispassionate towards the senses body mind and intellect, renounces the desire for the fruit of karm and works only for purification of the Inner-Self and attainment of Brahm. The one who is not a yogi, gets infatuated by desires.

»➤ What are the types of karm of a sankhya yogi, Prabho!

☀ A sankhya yogi who has control over body mind and senses, is neither a karta, doer, nor a kaaran, cause, is centred in himself.

»➤ If not the sankhya yogi, then Prabhu must be getting the karm done...

☀ No, humans do karm according to their swabhav, nature, and assume that they themselves are the karta...

- Due to this, automatically some association with the karmphal, fruit of karm, takes place
- The omnipresent Brahm is not party to the results of anyone's karm
- Due to ignorance the being who under the illusion that he is the karta-bhokta, doer and user, gets caught in the vicious circle of birth and death

- Destroy ignorance through wisdom
- Destroy doubts dualities and sins.

Wise sadhaks while alive attain Brahm, liberation, become Brahm-swaroop, Brahm like, and after life, merge with the peaceful Brahm.

»➤ What is the other way to attain liberation and Brahm-padd, Supreme State...

Dhyan yog — renouncing all external subjects; fixing the gaze in the middle of the brows; controlling the breath; equalising rechak poorak kumbhak, deep exhalation inhalation retention; keeping the mind and intellect in control; free from desire fear and anger; such a dhyan yogi sadhak is forever free.

»➤ Any other easier way, O Prabho!

Bhakti yog — the one who knows, accepts Prabhu to be the supreme well-wisher most compassionate 'loveful' selfless, such a person attains supreme bliss.

|| ॐ ||

Om Parmatmaney Namah
Shree Krishnam Vande Jagadgurum
Jai Yogeshwar

Wednesday, 3.2.1993   Time: Night 1.10
Om Bram Breem Brom Seh Buddhaye Namah

Chapter 6

Yog of Self-Discipline
Yog Practice and Dhyan

＊ *Ashtang Yog:*
*Yam * Niyam * Asan * Pranayam * Pratiyahaar*
*Dharna *Dhyan * Samadhi*

The human who remains unattached to the karmphal, result of his actions, without taking refuge in created and destructible things, does his kartavya karm, duty karm, such a person is a sanyasi and a yogi.

Karm is present in both: sanyas — sankhya yog, and karm yog

O Arjun, my mann, my heart...

The one who neither lights the fire for his own service nor performs karm, is not a yogi.

»➤ What is the mahima, greatness, of a sanyasi and a yogi...

☀ Without renouncing all his resolves and heart's desires a human is neither a yogi nor a sanyasi...

»➤ What is the cause and significance of being a yogi...

☀ For a yogi to perform duty-karm dispassionately is to be yogaroorh, centred in yog. Not savouring the peace gained from renouncing the world and consequently, performing karm is the way to achieve Supreme Tattve, essence.

»➤ What are the attribute of such a human... Prabho...

☀ The one who is not attached to karm and sankalp is yogaroorh, centred in yog.

»➤ How to be that...Prabho...

☀ One has to deliver himself on his own.

- The mind is one's own enemy and one's own friend
- Winning over oneself and connected to the truth, then the mind is a friend
- When no control on the self and connected to falsehood, then enemy

- Being your own friend and staying nirvikar, unsullied, under unfavourable-favourable circumstances, success-failure, respect-disrespect, are means to attain Supreme.

➤ What are the qualities of a person who has attained Supreme-hood...

☀ His antahkaran, Inner Being, is saturated with gyan-vigyan, knowledge and science.

- Has control over senses and under all circumstances stays nirvikar, unaffected
- Considers gold and stone alike, is equanimous not only towards objects but is dispassionate amidst benefactors friends enemies sinners saints and jealous ones. Such a person is a superb human.

➤ How to attain sambuddhi...

☀ Through dhyan yog also.

- A dhyan yogi renounces even from his mind, pleasures of the senses and accumulation of luxuries by being desireless
- Keeping his Inner-Self and body constrained and living alone in solitude, always joyous and keeps the self engrossed in Supreme.

»➤ What are the ways of dhyan...

☀ Sit in a clean, pure place, spreading a deer skin or a clean cloth. Be firm, unmoving and straight; the seat should not be high or low. Contract the actions of the intellect and sense organs. Keep the mind focussed.
For the purification of the inner being, practise dhyan yog...

- Hold the body straight in one line
- Watch the tip of the nose, sit motionless
- Devoid of fear and strife, firmly focus on Supreme
- Be in absolute surrender to Me, only then shall you attain sublime peace.

»➤ There are many such dhyan yogis but why are they not siddh, accomplished, O Prabho!

☀ Not the one who either eats and sleeps too much or too less; the dhyan yogi who has balanced food and is appropriate in his conduct, behaviour and thinking will become siddh...

- The one who moves around and acts in a judicious manner, he is a siddh
- The one who remains unaffected from sorrow or joy is a dhyan yogi

- When there is no desire or need for any object then the chit, intellect, is firm in its true self
- The state of the yogi's chit becomes like an unwavering flame of a lamp.

»➤ What is the state of the chit, inner feel, of a siddh yogi...

☀ It becomes like a flame that does not flicker at all...

- Unsullied pure unaffected peaceful in itself
- Absolutely content
- Being fully satisfied within, a yogi experiences unlimited bliss, beyond senses...
- Being established in such a real bliss, a dhyan yogi is never disturbed nor does he oscillate from his state
- Because there is no greater joy than this bliss
- The one who is established in this state is never affected by the greatest of great sorrow; such a yogi is never short of anand; distress does not touch him.

»➤ How to attain this state...Prabho!

☀ Absolute disconnect with the feel of agony and nonchalant towards the world. This nirukti, dispassion, is yog.

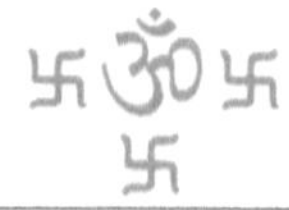

Without getting weary, with a determined mind attain such yog.

»➤ Some other way to attain such a yog and the resulting equanimity...

☀ Contemplate the nirgun and nirakaar, attributeless and formless.

- Renounce from the heart, all the desires that emerge from sankalps, pledges

- Withdraw the senses from everywhere with dhyan, then through the intellect gradually attain uparati, virakti and upram — renounce the world, getting disillusioned by it, recede from the world

- Keep the mind and heart fixed on Prabhu, don't contemplate anything other than Supreme

- A Brahm-swaroop yogi whose mind is removed from the rajasic tendencies is peaceful, sinless and attains the ultimate sattvic anand

- After that, being forever firmly focussed on Supreme, such a yogi experiences and attains absolute joy and bliss.

»➤ How does the one whose dhyan is forever focussed on the Self, view the world...

☀ He sees all beings in himself and in all beings sees himself. He is samdarshi, views everyone in the same way, nirgun and nirakaar. The one who worships the sagun-sakaar, the manifested form, sees Supreme in all and all in Supreme.

»➤ Why are you and such a yogi not invisible to each other...

☀ I am prevailing in all creatures, knowing this he worships me only and remains constantly and consistently fixed on me. Then, how is it possible to be invisible to him.

- A nirgun nirakaar dhyan yogi stays the same in joy and in sorrow, sees himself in all creatures, hence is sarvshreshth, the best.

»➤ How to tame the fickle mind...

☀ It is possible through practise and abstinence.

When the mind and senses are under control it is possible to accomplish dhyan yog.

»➤ What is the state in case the effort slackens, Prabho!

☀ There is no denouement as the aim is welfare.

- But such a person spends time on higher planes like Swarg Lok for a few years and then is born again in Mrityu Lok, the earthly plane, in the house of a genuine gentleman, because the desire for worldly comforts still lingers on

- Being mostly desireless but soiled at the last moment due to some reason, such a sadhak takes birth straightaway in the home of a tattvagya, knower of the essence...this birth is rare. The resources to complete his incomplete task are arranged effortlessly
- Being born in a gentleman's home, due to his previous spiritual practice, his dhyan is automatically drawn to the Supreme Master. Because of this he quickly commences his sadhna and attains the supreme status very fast.

»➤ What is the stature of the one who attains the supreme status...

❈ He is an ultimate yogi, greater than the wise men who perform rituals like hawans and yagyas, and tapasvies who undergo penance with sakaam bhav, with a motive.

That is why O Arjun, be a yogi.

❋ *Do as instructed by the Supreme Master, O meena manu...*

»➤ Amongst yogis, who is the ultimate...

The one who is totally absorbed in me in full surrender, always sings with faith the hymns in my glory... Such a devotee of mine is superb amongst all yogis.

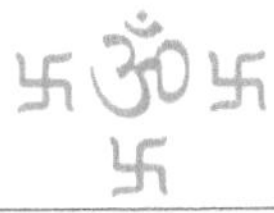

Om Parmatmaney Namah
Shree Krishnam Vande Jagadgurum
Jai Yogeshwar

Wednesday, 3.2.1993   Time: Night 2.45

Om Bram Breem Brom Seh Buddhaye Namah

Chapter 7

Supreme is the Truth
Wholistic Gyan

➤ To become the best yogi...

✷ Engrossed in me and taking shelter in me, always chanting my name, you will realise my complete form, including its gyan and vigyan, knowledge and science. Knowing that after which nothing remains to be known.

➤ How...

✷ Will impart the gyan of this to you.

- All humans cannot know my absolute form, fathom or relate to it because it is not their natural inclination. For their own welfare and evolution of the soul, hardly one in thousands endeavours to know me and among those who try, rarely one is capable of realising my samagra roop, whole and complete form, through essence

- Samagra roop — my wholistic sublime highest human form — the ultimate sublime form of Supreme Being
- Earth water fire air ether mind intellect and ego, these eight comprise my apara, worldly materialistic gross nature
- Completely different from this is my nature that manifests from para consciousness. To nurture the world, it reflects attachment in the form of mine and thine
- The union of para and apara is the cause of creation of beings
- I am the sole purpose of the entire world
- The world sprouts from me and dissolves into me
- Just like beads strung in a thread and the thread in all beads, I am in all beings.

I Am That

I am the rasa, liquidity in the water; the
effulgence and luminosity in the sun
and the moon
I am Om, pranav in the Veds
The shabd, sound in the sky

True purushaarth, endeavour in humans
The pure fragrance in the Earth
The sparkle in the fire
The life force in all beings
The eternal seed of all beings
I am the penance of tapasvis, hermits ascetics
The intelligence in the intelligent
The brightness in the bright
The aspiration in the strong
I am kaam, lust in humans, which is in
accordance with Dharm, righteousness
I am the sattvic force that is devoid of
attachment
I am in all.

- All sattvic rajasic and tamasic bhav are in me
  but I am detached and beyond them eternally
  constantly forever...

➤ Why don't people understand you like this,
Prabho...

☀ The reason why people don't know me thus is
because they are allured by the world created by
satva rajas and tamas.

➤ O Prabho! Who can know you...

☀ The ones who have taken refuge in me by turning
away from the maya of the three gunas, becoming

gunateet, rising above the gunas through complete surrender.

»➤ Then why don't all come in your surrender ...

※ Because of taking refuge in the aasuri bhav, satanic feel, maya clouds their knowledge and wisdom

»➤ Who are in your surrender...

※ These are as follows —

- Artharthi, those wanting wealth...
- Aart, those who are in agony
- Jigyasu, the curious ones
- Gyani-premi, knowledgeable and loving ones
- All four kinds of devotees, performing good karm, take refuge in me through dhyan and bhajan
- Amongst these four, though all are good and loved by me, the wise, loving person with ananya bhakti, unflinching devotion, is extremely dear to me.

»➤ What is so special about the 'loveful' devotee...

※ He is like a reflection of my soul.

- He has supreme unshakeable faith in me
- Artharthi has desire for wealth

- Aart has desire to get rid of agonies
- Jigyasu has the desire to know the essence
- Gyani-premi feels that Vasudev is everything. He, who knows, assumes and feels thus, such a mahatma is rare in this world.

»➤ What about those in whom this wisdom is covered...

☀ They take refuge in other devtas and worship them for the fulfilment of their desires.

»➤ Why do you not pull them towards your Being...

☀ I do not take away the freedom of choice given to humans...

- Whosoever is engrossed in whatever deity, I strengthen his belief in the same
- However, the vidhaan, dispensation of the result, is mine alone
- I cannot be attained by the ordinary devotee with an inferior mind
- They get perishable results that are bound by birth and dissolution
- Their reach is till devlok, the abode of devtas
- However, my devotees attain me alone.

»➤ Then why everyone is not your devotee...

☀ The unintelligent consider me as a mere mortal bound by birth and death.

➤ Why do you not tell, reveal your real form...

☀ Covered by yogmaya, illusions of the world, I do not show my true form.

- I know all creatures born in the past present and future, but the creatures infatuated by maya do not know me
- The main reason for not knowing me is the strife that arises from jealousy resentment and affectation. Being confused and indulgent, these creatures remain stuck in the cycle of birth and death
- Everyone does not remain infatuated. Those with virtuous deeds have destroyed their sins become free from duality and concentrate on me. Aek vrati, having a single-minded resolve, determined, they focus on me.

➤ What happens by having an unshakeable resolve of your dhyan...

☀ They get to know about the Brahm, poorn adhyatm, complete spirituality, complete karm and the gyan and science of the entire creation.

- They realise my whole being. 'Vasudev' is everything, knowing this they attain me. At the time of their end, they dissolve in me.

✻ *In every yug, whoever imparts sadbuddhi, good senses, the highest wisdom and delivers the world, he is an Avtar. According to the yugs and their evolution, Avtars too evolve but their core attributes remain the same.*

That Brahm Gyan, voice of the soul and knowledge of Self-realisation, keeps getting enhanced but the base is the same wisdom and truth, Supreme Truth. Only the ways of attaining telling and explaining it keep changing forms.

|| ॐ ||

What is Supreme Truth

This knowledge is bestowed only upon the one on whom that greatest power, the Supreme Soul — Param Tattve is benevolent.

Gratitude for being fortunate to have a human form...

For Gyan, knowledge
Smriti, sharp memory
Buddhi, intellect
Chintan, contemplation
Mannan, meditation
Smaran, remembrance.

If not for this body mind and intellect, how could one have awakened the vivek, wisdom to attain Supreme Bliss. By awakening of wisdom, Vasudev is attained. If Vasudev exists...he is here...is here...is here... This is Supreme Truth.

This is Supreme Truth

You are not you
I am not me
He is not he
This is not this
Everything has become ONE...merged.
This very moment is supreme bliss
This is the only wealth that once received
Never leaves.
Am blessed, O Supreme, Eeshwar
Glory to Shree Krishn...

|| ॐ ||

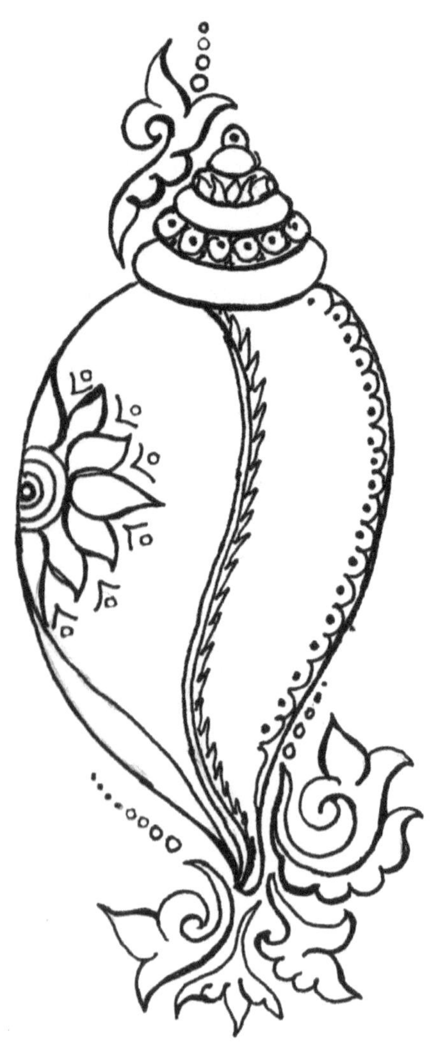

Om Parmatmaney Namah
Shree Krishnam Vande Jagadgurum
Jai Yogeshwar

Wednesday, 7.4.1993   Time: Evening 4.45
Om Bram Breem Brom Seh Buddhaye Namah

Chapter 8

Unflinching Devotion – Supreme Yog

»➤ What is Brahm, O Bhagwan!

☀ That eternal formless attribute-less Supreme is Brahm.

»➤ What is spirituality...

☀ The truth of the existence of the being is spirituality.

»➤ What is the karm of Brahm...

☀ During Pralaya, the great deluge, all beings merge into my being. I manifest them in the beginning of a yug to make them go through the consequences of their karm; providing them with a particular body to which they can relate, is my dispassionate karm.

»➤ Prabho! What is adhibhoot...

☀ Things which are perishable.

»➤ What is adhidaiv...

☀ The emanation of the first Supreme Being — Brahma is adhidaiv.

»➤ What is adhiyagya...

☀ In this body, the invisible form that is 'I' (Vasudev) is adhiyagya.

- In the last moments, whoever remembers me, merges in me
- So the feel at the last moment is most significant.

»➤ How to recall the Supreme in the final moments...

☀ Remember Prabhu all the time.

- Along with that perform the duty-karm bestowed upon you on its own accord. This is the mahamantra, greatest mantra.

»➤ What form or projection of yours should one contemplate on, O Prabhu...

❋ Sagun-nirakaar, with qualities and formless

Nirgun-nirakaar, without qualities and formless

Sagun-sakaar, with attributes and form.

All three are reflections of my being. The human who practises yog sadhna with unflinching bhav, feel, and leaves the body remembering the formless Divine Being, he merges with the same.

»➤ How is that being...

❋ Omniscient, reigning over all from the beginning.

- Subtler than subtlest, provider of all beyond imagination, completely devoid of ignorance and darkness, luminous like the sun, Being of Light. Concentrating between the brows and contemplating on this form, the human soul attains Supreme Divine Being after leaving the body.

The first way to contemplate the Divine:

Sagun–nirakaar

- To attain daiveeye gunas, divine attributes of Supreme Being, is quite difficult but not impossible. The aim of the human body should be to acquire these sublime gunas

- Only then the being is Brahm — Aham Brahmasmi
- All have same prakash, luminosity
- I am in all...

This realisation will dawn
This bhav, feel, will prevail.

The second way to ponder over the Divine:

Nirgun — Nirakaar

- A sadhak is known as the knower of Veds and the eternal Brahm, who in his last moments is able to take the prana established in his heart to the crown. A human immersed in yog sadhna reciting Om, the eternal sound of Brahm, meditating upon the nirgun-nirakaar is able to let go of his prana, he attains moksha, Param Gati, the Supreme State.

The third way to contemplate:

Sagun-Sakaar

- The one with the thoughts of my being alone, full of absolute love for me will effortlessly attain me, be freed of bondage of birth and death
- By reaching other lokas, planes, one has to come back, but after merging in me, this cycle ends.

»➤ Why other lokas are repetitive...

Bound by time limits according to human calculations, one day and night of Brahma is equivalent to one thousand cycles of four yugas. Creation happens in the day and at night all is dissolved in Brahm. The ones with raag-dvesh, indulgence jealousy resentment go on repeating this cycle of coming and going.

»➤ What is imperishable, better than this unseen Brahm.

The best is Paraatpar Brahm, Supreme Sublime — that is constant consistent Supreme Soul which is omnipresent in the form of bhav, feel.

- This is the Param Atma, Supreme Soul; Brahm gyan, absolute gyan; tattve gyan, the essence of gyan that never perishes
- Only gyan eliminates darkness
- Mansa vacha karmana satya, thoughts speech and deeds tied with the same Truth. Say that which you think and do the same
- This real truthful gyan of Param Atma does not perish even when all the creatures are destroyed
- That is defined as unmanifested eternal indestructable and Param Gati

- This is the ultimate dhaam, abode from where no one returns

- After attaining the sampoorn gyan, complete gyan, there is nothing left to be known.

✷ *Through unwavering, constant bhakti, the eternal abode is attained.*
Through total perseverance gyan is attained.

☀ After death there are two paths of coming and going:

- Uttarayan — the six-month-long northern path; that of fire in the form of light; waxing moon; ruled by devtas, divine deities. Those who have realised the Brahm take this path, never to return
- Dakshinayan — the southern path; that of the dark night; Krishn paksh, waning moon; ruled by its reigning deities
- Those who are sakaam, with desires for fruits of karm take this path to go and enjoy the sukh or pleasures of swarg, heaven, and thereafter return
- Both the paths have been there since the beginning of Creation
- The only solution is to be detached and not indulge in the world.

✳ *Always be dispassionate, do not exceedingly indulge in this world, O Human.*

A soulful yogi who knows Thy true essence alone attains the eternal plane, the Paramatma tattve – the essence of Supreme Being.

|| ॐ ||

Om Parmatmaney Namah

Shree Krishnam Vande Jagadgurum

Jai Yogeshwar

Wednesday, 14.4.1993   Time: Night 2.13

Om Bram Breem Brom Seh Buddhaye Namah

Chapter 9

Divine Wisdom

O Arjun, since you are never jealous of me, I shall state to you this extremely secretive gyan and realisation, knowing which you shall become free of all turmoil and vexation...

Knowledge with its science is the sovereign of all spheres and secrets. Extremely pure, superb and with evident results, this knowledge liberates one from worldly trials. It is absolutely Parmatm-maye, saturated with the feel of Supreme Soul; Dharm-maye, rightful; imperishable and extremely accessible.

The human, because of lack of faith in the eternal sanatan dharm, experiences repeated births and deaths, continues to live and die in this lifetime too.

➤ Who is the base and the creator of this world...

Even though I am the creator retainer and preserver of all beings, I am poorntaya nirlipt, absolutely detached.

Just like air is ever present in the sky, similarly all beings are in me. They dissolve in me at the time of Pralaya, the great deluge. I recreate them when it is time for Creation to begin.

- I am Supreme Consciousness, Supreme Energy; Param Tattve, Supreme Essence
- Creating repeatedly does not tie me down because that karm is performed without any attachment, with complete dispassion and absolute wisdom
- Through energy power and inspiration, my reign creates matter and beings. It is due to my presiding factor that various changes take place in the world.

Even then, why don't people place their faith in you...

The moorh, ignorant people, take me to be an ordinary human being and ignore me.

- People with aasuri, demonic alluring tendencies and imbecile nature, are liars
- The aspirations good deeds and knowledge of such moorh people are a waste and without truthful results
- The ones who know me as aadi-anadi, with no beginning no end; avinashi, eternal

invincible; and abide by the daivik sampada, divine virtues; keep faith in me and are devoted to me, they attain me. Bhakti yog is to be always engrossed in me, with the intellect that has a one-point focus, to attain me

- Gyan Yog — gyan yogis know that the entire world is a manifestation of my form and revere me.

  It is I who is the amrit and death; truth-falsehood; matter-being; creation-dissolution; rules-legislations; initiator; yagya; swadha, offerings; aushadhi, medicine; ghee; mantra and fire.

  I am a form of hawan...

  I am the mechanism, purity of the four Veds. I am the father mother guardian grandfather provider; gati, pace; saakshi, witness; Supreme Abode, refuge, deluge and the indestructible seed.

➤ If you are everything, then why do people worship others...

☀ Those with desires for sukh and luxuries worship devtas; they are repeatedly born and die.

- The ones who take refuge in me, I bear the responsibility of their yogkshem, sadhna and welfare

- I alone am the Master of the entire universe
- The ones who do not realise this tattve of mine, they fall from grace
- The one who is devoted to a certain deity, he will reach the same
- Worshipping me is the easiest. Offer everything to me; by this one will be freed from bearing karmphal, results of one's karm
- I am present equally in all beings
- But especially present in those ananya bhakt, unique devotees, who have absolute faith in me
- I accept everything, even leaves flowers fruits... offered by them
- Even the amoral one taking right decisions and following the righteous path will reach me
- My devotee will never fall from grace.
  Anyone, of any gunas, attributes, taking refuge in my worship can attain me.
      Be of my mann, understanding
        By becoming my devotee
          By taking refuge in me
          By worshipping me
    You shall come unto me...attain me.
      In all creatures, I am the same
    Neither do I love nor resent anyone
  But those who remember me with love
    I am in them and they are in me.

✳ *Bhavpoorn hai sakal srishti – the whole creation runs on bhav, the underlying thoughts and feels of actions.*

Our world is created through these. Have faith in your sankalps, resolves and maintain 'ek nishchaye wali buddhi,' mind with one-point programme. Be in absolute surrender then Param Bodhi, Supreme Intelligence will arrange everything to fulfil that resolve. Strong and constant connection with the Supreme, empowers dhyan for receiving messages and directives for right karm according to the time requirement.

|| ॐ ||

ॐ

Om Parmatmaney Namah
Shree Krishnam Vande Jagadgurum
Jai Yogeshwar

Tuesday, 25.5.1993   Time: Night 8.30
Om Bram Breem Brom Seh Buddhaye Namah

Chapter 10

Divine Attributes

Since you are my greatest friend and love me immensely, to you I will state my Supreme Truth. This world has been manifested by me. I am the origin of all gyanis, wise ones. The one who knows me as Eeshwar, unmanifest eternal imperishable, the master of all worlds, is delivered from all sins. Fear-fearlessness, non-violence, equanimity, contentment, penance-charity, fame-infamy, honour-dishonour; all bhav, feels, arise from me, as do all deities — four Sankadiks, fourteen Manus, seven Saptrishis.

- The creator nurturer and teacher of all...
  All of this I am
  I alone am.

* *One of the capacities of Prabhu is yog — merging with all.*

From this yog, other attributes of Bhagwan are realised.

I am the root cause of the whole world.
All the efforts of the world are my forms.

- Knowing this wisdom my unique unwavering devotees, the intelligent ones with focussed intellect, love me alone
- Forever content, they love and worship me only
- For such devotees, Buddhi Yog, attaining equanimity, becomes the cause to attain Me.

Light the lamp of wisdom by annihilating ignorance.

All insightful divine seers know you alone as Vibhu, the all-pervasive One.
Thou art the manifestation of Truth, this I believe.
Only you know thyself.
All that is majestic illustrious noble and divine are vibhutis, reflections of you...

I am the origin and end of all creatures.
It is me alone... the Soul; Vishnu; the son of Aditi, Vaman... all the Avtars.
Sun Moon Shiv Kuber fire mountains water Ved and Guru Brihaspati...

I am that.

Among words I am Pranam, Pranav.

Among trees I am peepal, among mantras the Gayatri. Narad Chitrarath Kapil muni Uchchaishrava Airavat... all these are my vibhutis, divine glories.

Vasuki Sheshnag Kamdhenu Kamdev Varun Aryama Prahlad Garuda Ganga Yamraj...

I am that.

I am at the start and end of yugas.

In spiritual discourses, I am the argument and counter-argument, I am also the Tattve Nirnayak, decisive factor of the true essence.

I am Mahakaal of Kaal, the Supreme Destroyer of destruction itself...

It is me alone.

In birth-death; in female-male; in keerti, fame; shree, glory; speech; memory; medha, intelligence; dhriti, intellect; and in forgiveness...

It is me alone.

Gayatri in mantras, Margshish in months, Vasant ritu, Spring, among seasons. Gambling, effulgence victory decision and sattvic bhav, feel

I am that.

Among the Pandavs I am Dhananjay, among the Vrishnis I am Vasudev, Ved Vyas in munis, Shukracharya in poets, wisdom in the wise, punishment in oppression,

Niti, law of righteousness, in those who aspire for victory....

Silence in the secret bhav, feel, I am prevalent in all matter and being as a bhav, seed...
I am everything, I am much more too.
Movable-immovable, everything I am.
In the world whatever is full of opulence grace and power, has my effulgence and reflection, know this gyan.

✳ *All those Superb Humans connected to the Supreme Consciousness who have come before and will come after Dwapar yug will be the reflection of that Supreme. There is no end to the divine reflections of the Supreme Being.*

|| ॐ ||

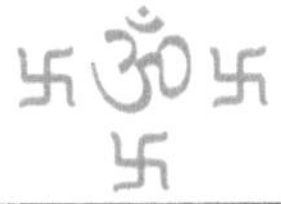

Om Parmatmaney Namah
Shree Krishnam Vande Jagadgurum
Jai Yogeshwar

Wednesday, 26.5.1993   Time: Night 1.25
Om Bram Breem Brom Seh Buddhaye Namah

Chapter 11

Vision of Cosmic Form

I am at the root, base of all. My being is the origin, the source of everything. The moment this wisdom dawns, attachment ignorance dissipate.

Prabho! Show your Parameshwar, Supreme Form, Virat Roop that is imperishable...

I have hundreds and thousands of forms and all are divine. These have not been seen before, besides these if there is anything else, you can see that too...

How to see, Prabho...

With divya-chakshu, divine eyes, see all the potentialities related to the Divine! See the Divya Darshan, divine form of Supreme...

Thousands of faces hands eyes and sublime ornaments, weapons held in numerous hands, as if thousands of suns have appeared all at once; crores of universes have come together in one fragment.

Sanjay: Wonderstruck Arjun gets goose bumps, starts eulogising, glorifying...

»➤ O Master!
O Vishwa Roop, Cosmic Form
O Vishveshwar, Lord of the Universe
You are the imperishable Brahm...
You are the foundation of the universe and the entire world...
You are the absolute, eternal purush who is the protector of the sanatan, eternal imperishable dharm. All devtas asuras maharishis and all of the Siddh Samudaaye, community of evolved, perfect souls are extolling your glory. I am petrified seeing this form of yours...

Sanjay: Prabhu is showing all sins, sinners of the Kaurav clan, Bheeshm Drona and other gurus... going into the gigantic mouth of Kaal, time. The aggressive luminosity of Prabhu's light is filling the entire world, afflicting everyone. Thus, Prabhu revealed — "I am Kaal, the destroyer of all lokas, planes, descended on the Earth at this time."

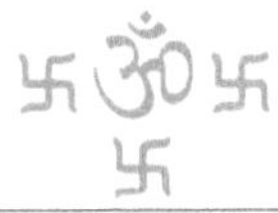

»➤ Why are you here O Master...

❋ For the purpose of establishing dharm.

At this time I am here to annihilate all sinners, and to give and receive love, too.

O Arjun! Become a medium... all these people are already dead, all of them have already been killed by me.

O Savyasaachin, Ambidextrous One, you are a mere cause...

You shall achieve victory over all enemies in the war.

Sanjay: Arjun is reciting Prabhu stuti, eulogising Prabhu, full of feel from the depth of his soul. Teary-eyed...

»➤ You are the divine manifested form of the Imperishable.

Satt-asatt, truth-falsehood; the Guru of Gurus; the primordial deity Vishnu; Puran Purush; the basis of the world. You are every thing. Obeisance to you...

You are All.

Pranam to you, namaskar to you over and over again. Not knowing this greatness of yours, I treated you like a mere friend, fought with you.

Pardon me, O Prabho!

Now what do you want Arjun...

➤ Having witnessed your divine form, feeling very delighted; now please give darshan of your Vishnu form — the chaturbhuj roop, four-armed form with chakra, discus; gada, mace; shankh, conch; and padam, lotus.

The form that has been revealed to you, no one can see it even through jap tap sadhna, chanting penance and spiritual practice.
Now see my that very chaturbhuj form. See...see it... whole and complete...
Then again Prabhu appeared in his gentle two-armed human form relieving Arjun of his fear...

➤ Now I am at ease, Prabhu...

The chaturbhuj roop is visible only through ananya, unflinching, bhakti and not through any other vidha, mode.
It can be realised and known through tattve gyan.

➤ What is ananya bhakti, Prabhu...

Samta yog, yog of equanimity:

- Doing every deed, karm, for me

- Taking refuge in only me
- Being my devotee alone
- Free from attachments
- Having no animosity towards anyone, this is the path of devotion. The one who is full of such devotion comes to me.

✳ *Manu meena also realised this through tattve gyan... This is truth, manu's truth, whether anyone agrees or not... meena has become Prabhumayee, Krishnamayee... full of Prabhu and Krishn...*

Eeshwar is the truth
Come all take refuge in this very Truth Love Karm
and Light...
This is Truth
Truth is here.

|| 卐 ||

Krishn is the Name of the All-Pervading Energy

Krishn is the name of the all-pervading energy
Krishn is an adjective for the qualities
Of this all-pervading energy
The qualities of this energy are
Omnipotence
Omniscience
Omnipresence
Satyam shivam sunderam —
Truthful, for welfare of all, beautiful
Only the blessed ones will recognise...
meena is grateful to the brain
that could see beyond...

Give give give like Nature
Evolve evolve evolve like Nature
Until poorn absolute yog happens
No duality remains
Where Supreme Will is your will
Your will is Supreme Will
Love love love love
Love is Supreme.

|| 卐 ||

Om Parmatmaney Namah

Shree Krishnam Vande Jagadgurum

Jai Yogeshwar

Wednesday, 9.6.1993   Time: Night 1.10

Om Bram Breem Brom Seh Buddhaye Namah

Chapter 12

Yog of Devotion

➤ Who is a better devotee, the one who worships the form or the formless...

➤ Those devotees who, with complete faith, believe in me worship me and do intense meditative veneration are the best worshippers...

- Worshippers of the formless, who having disciplined all senses, are unflinching, absolutely centred in the higher self, not directed otherwise, know that Pranav, the eternal Om, is dhruv satya, the established truth, they too attain Supreme

- Those who offer all their karm, deeds to me are anchored in me, they are redeemed faster.

➤ How to become such a devotee...

Engage your mann, heart and mind, only in me...
Through abhyas yog, yog of practise, aspire to attain me.
If this is not possible then do all karm for me.
Even if this is not possible then adopt bhakti yog.
Renounce sampoorn karmphal, fruit of entire karm.

So, is surrendering karmphal the lowest recourse...

No, Arjun...

- Shastra gyan, knowledge of scriptures, is better than mechanically and habitually performing rituals without internalising the wisdom behind them
- Dhyan that happens naturally is better than knowledge of scriptures that have not been internalised, therefore, not resulting in yog, merging with the Divine
- But if the dhyan becomes mere meditation, mechanical and does not lead to yog, state of merging with the Divine, it is better to perform karm that comes in front by being detached and consciously surrendering the karmphal to the Divine.

What are the characteristics of a siddh, realised devotee who has attained you...

No dvesh, resentment for anyone...

- Always friendly, compassionate and merciful towards all
- Beyond the feelings of mine and thine, forgiving and maintaining placidity in grief and joy
- Body senses and mind under control. Such a determined one is dear to me
- The human who has a one-point programme, is full of knowledge, is wise and logical is dear to me
- The human by whom others are not disturbed, the one who is not bothered by intense sensations, nor is he overcome by jealousy fear joy and anger, such a person is endowed with my attributes; he is my ansh, particle, and is dear to me
- Who does not have any desire for any object nor company, pure from inside and outside, efficient, clever, performs only that karm for which the human body has been bestowed — to attain Supreme
- Detached from the world, calm at heart, distant from the tendency to luxuriate and hoard, such a person can attain me, understand me
- He is mine and I am in him
- The one who is same in favourable and unfavourable periods, neither excited nor depressed, feels no difference between auspicious and inauspicious, he alone is dear to me

- Same with enemy-friend, honour-dishonour... detached, takes criticism and praise as the same, introspective, self-motivated, doing self-study, a yogi who is content in sustaining the body in any way
- Devoid of any fascination for the dwelling place or the body
- The one with such a steadfast mind is dear to me.

✳ *Those who suffer from afflictions are also dear to me because they are unwell, they need prayers — may Prabhu bestow upon them good senses, only then shall they recognise me and their suffering will dissipate.*

To get angry and curse is not appropriate.
To reform is my karm
Everyone is dear to me
The whole world is my abode
I am in all homes, in all hearts
Great benevolence of the Creator
Eeshwar is the truth.

This is Truth
Truth is here.

|| ॐ ||

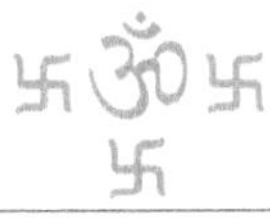

Om Parmatmaney Namah

Shree Krishnam Vande Jagadgurum

Jai Yogeshwar

Wednesday, 16.6.1993   Time: Night 1.00

Om Bram Breem Brom Seh Buddhaye Namah

Chapter 13

The Medium of Karm and its Knower

Those who worship the nirgun and nirakaar, the one without any attributes and form, are wise ones.

Why are they wise, Bhagwan...

Because they know the kshetra, field, and kshetragya, knower of the field, as 'yeh roop', this form, and witness it as 'that'.

This body is called kshetra, field. And the one who knows this kshetra is known as kshetragya.

Shareer is the physical body and shareeri is the knower or witness 'to the body'.

Shareer is kshetra and shareeri is kshetragya. I am in all kshetras, bodies, and kshetragya, shareeri forms. To know understand and realise this is true gyan.

It is I who am in all — Paragyanam Brahm.

- Kshetra comprises twenty-four elements — the mool prakriti, inherent nature; samashti buddhi, integrated intellect; aham tattve, ego; the five mahabhoota, elements; ten senses, indriyas; one mann, heart-mind; and the five emotions — kaam krodh lobh moh and ahankaar, lust anger greed attachment and ego.
It has seven reflections:
Iccha, desire; dvesh, resentment; dukh, sorrow; sukh, happiness; shareer, body; pran shakti, breath energy; and dhaarn shakti, retention power.

⟫➤ With which bhav can this body be felt as THAT...

✺ The means through which the body can be seen as such are these:

- Absence of abhiman, arrogance of being superior
- No showing-off and artificial behaviour
- Not giving even the slightest pain to anyone through body mind and speech
- Forgiving nature
- Simplicity of thought words and deeds
- Serving gurus to attain gyan
- Purity of the body and Inner-Self
- Not getting distracted from ones goal

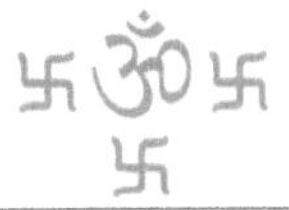

- Keeping the mind in control under all circumstances
- Being detached from the subjects of senses
- No egotism
- Knowing and understanding the root cause of all sorrows — birth death old-age and diseases — for detachment
- Dispassionate
- Not engrossed in relations relatives objects home belongings
- Always maintaining equanimity under favourable and unfavourable circumstances
- Merging in me with ananya bhakti, unparallel single-minded devotion
- Unflinching faith in me is yog, merging, being centred in me
- Seeking solitude and being solitary by nature
- Not allured by crowds
- Contemplating and meditating on the Supreme Entity regularly constantly consistently
- Always seeing His reflection and reign everywhere. Witnessing the body as 'yeh roop' as THAT, separate from oneself, is gyan. Taking this body as your own form is ignorance.

»➤ What is the essence attained from this gyan...

✷ Paramatma, the Supreme Soul, is the gyey tattve, that which is knowable. It is Param Brahm, infinite and eternal...

- Neither true nor false, prevailing in all and everywhere; many contrary elements too are immersed in THAT...
- Even then there is no contradiction within
- Though being One, pervades in all fluidly
- Creator of Deluge and Creation, nurturer and provider, and annihilator — realise that is Paramatma, Supreme Soul.

❋ *Know that He resides in every heart. There exists no other reign besides His. Viraat Roop, the grandiose form; Laghu Roop, the tiniest form; the illuminating gyan form, these alone are his swaroop, true forms.*

Your breath is His Pran, life breath.

His breath is your breath.

Renounce arrogance.

You are THAT Tattve, essence.

To the practitioner of the path of knowledge, knowing the difference between prakriti and purush, kshetra and kshetragya is very essential.

- Good qualities and imperfections are bestowed by Nature

  Kaarya-karan, deeds and their performer; the kaaran and kartapan, reason and the ability to perform them are also conferred by Nature.

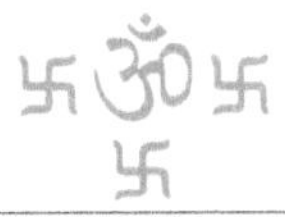

Based on their individual nature, men and women perform deeds

- But only that person is regarded as a great soul who although in human form is free from the ties of the body
- Knowing the swaroop of prakriti and purush, performing actions according to the dharm and scriptures, the human can be liberated from the fear of birth and death.

»➤ What are the ways of knowing the true form, Prabho...

☀ Dhyan yog karm yog sankhya yog.

The easiest way is to take refuge in the liberated souls and obey and follow what they state.

»➤ How to be liberated from fear and the cycle of birth and death ...

☀ By recognising the relation of the soul with Paramatma, the Supreme Soul who is swatah siddh, instinctively axiomatic, and by snapping all ties with the body and its nature...

- Do not assume yourself to be dead with the death of the body
- Due to this one attains param-gati, Paramatma, the supreme state of the Supreme Soul.

»➤ How to snap the relationship with the body...

✳ All processes are under Nature's control.

- When a human understands that all the different creatures, their bhav, feel; their shareer, bodies; have all sprouted from the same Nature and are also firmly established in it, at that time he attains Brahm, the Supreme Self

- With the Brahm gyan, knowledge of the Brahm, the attachment to the body is gone, the connection dissipates. He realises that he is neither the karta, doer, nor the bhokta, user. He does not remain indulgent towards the body

- Just like space, even though it pervades everywhere, being extremely subtle, it is not engrossed in any person or object, similarly, this kshetragya, even though it permeates everything, remains unattached from the body, just like the sun which illumines everyone without the feel of a creator.

✳ *Through eyes of wisdom recognise Prabhu*
your soul and the Supreme Soul.
This very gyan jyoti, light of wisdom,
is Darshan, revelation.
This is the truth

Know it recognise it just become truthful

Become truthful in thought word and deed

Become 'loveful' become dutiful
Without the sense of doership
Just be a satyachari, practise truth
become truthful and attain Prabhu.

This is Truth
Truth is here.

|| ॐ ||

Om Parmatmaney Namah
Shree Krishnam Vande Jagadgurum
Jai Yogeshwar

Wednesday, 23.6.1993   Time: Night 1.44

Om Bram Breem Brom Seh Buddhaye Namah

Chapter 14

Gyan of Three Gunas of Nature

The gyan, knowing which all contemplative meditative humans attained param siddhi, sublime perfection; neither get perturbed even during the time of Mahapralaya, the great deluge, nor take birth even at the time of Mahasarg, the great re-creation of the new world; attain my dharm; now stating that gyan:

I am the father of all beings
I am the mother of all beings
Raj Tam Satt bind the bearer to the body...

- Satt Gunn is illuminating and flawless. However, due to its attachment to sukh, happiness and knowledge, it ties the dehi to the deh, owner of the body to the body

- Raj Gunn is raag, passion, passion for material things. So it gives rise to craving and infatuation and binds one to the longing for karmphal, the result of karm

- Tam Gunn emerges from ignorance and ties one to pramaad, inertia slothfulness slumber and laziness
- Satogunn gets the human involved in sukh and controls him. Rajogunn does the same through karm, while Tamogunn camouflages wisdom and ties human to pramaad, thus grips him. One guna rises by suppressing the other two
- When a human has absolute purity of the body mind and senses along with a strong urge to know the truth then it is Satogunn
- When driven by the desire for money comforts hoarding jealousy and competitiveness then it is Rajogunn
- When the inner being has been shadowed by moha, allurements and there exists frightful amount of laziness and one performs undesirable deeds then know that there is predominance of Tamogunn
- According to gunas the birth yoni, species, is ascertained:
Uttam lok, eminent plane — Satogunn
Manav lok, human plane — Rajogunn
Pashu lok, animal plane — Tamogunn

The result of a sattvic deed is pure.

The result of a rajasic one is sorrow inducing.

Tamasic karm leads to ignorance, dreadful hell

- Satt Gunn emerges from gyan, wisdom
- Raj Gunn erupts from greed
- Tam Gunn arises from ignorance and pramaad, infatuation
- The viveki, wise one, who realises that he is above and beyond the gunas, merges into my being
- Satt Gunn by nature turns towards prakash, light
- Raj Gunn is inclined towards bhog, luxuries of life
- Tam Gunn is inclined towards moh, attachments.

➻ Who attains you, Prabho...

✴ A gunateet, the one who is beyond these three aspects, transcends these gunas, attains me. He maintains equilibrium in happiness and sorrow; considers gold and dust as the same; and is above like-dislike, pleasant-unpleasant.

This Bhakti yog is possible through yog abhyas only.

- Attaining the Brahm is possible only through this, my dear friend, understand this

- Brahm, sanatan, eternal, amrit dharm and the refuge for all the sukh is in me alone. All are my forms and names

A Gunateet Human:

- The conduct of a gunateet human — he treats everyone equally, is patient composed and always centred in his true self
- Dispassionate in happiness-grief, gold-stone, criticism-praise, honour-dishonour, friend-foe, without desire and attachment, does not make new karm bondages
- Established in unparalleled bhakti yog, always engrossed in the simran, remembrance of Prabhu. Only that one becomes gunateet by transcending Satt Raj and Tam gunas.

✻ *There has been a shower of benevolence, meena has got immersed... Really, am I this worthy that Prabhu is giving Darshan, revealing the wisdom and my being is able to describe it! Darshan and true gyan, both are the same. Truth is Eshwar — Satyeshwar.*

> *This is Truth*
> *Truth is here.*

|| ꣼ ||

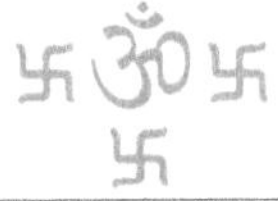

Om Parmatmaney Namah
Shree Krishnam Vande Jagadgurum
Jai Yogeshwar

Wednesday, 30.6.1993   Time: Night 2.45
Om Bram Breem Brom Seh Buddhaye Namah

Chapter 15

Gyan of Supreme Essence
I Alone Am in All — Sublime Human

✳ *Had an illuminating experience... sublime darshan*

Hari darshan, Prabhu darshan... the eye of wisdom opened

Blessed by the activation of the third eye

A thousandfold gratitude... Even the word 'gratitude' became insignificant.

⇒ If you are the basis of Brahm, then who is the basis of this world...

☀ I am the aadhaar, foundation of all.

- I am the base and refuge of this world which is akin to a tree

- Its roots are turned upwards and its branches and leaves are spreading downwards; its beginning and end are unknown
- The one who knows the reality of this tree of the world also knows the Veds. The knower of Veds is not ahankari, arrogant, but atmabali, with soul power.

❇ *The cellular memory that is eternal and constant becomes cause for Brahm to create. The whole world is its expansion, off-shoots and leaves.*

Raj Tam Satt gunas are the three branches of this worldly tree that are spread in all lokas, planes.

Speech touch taste smell and vision are their five tender leaves.

Contemplation is sprouting of new tender leaves.

The root is the manushya lok, human plane, because the effect of karm performed here impacts all the planes.

By cutting the branches of kaamna, aspirations; moh, attachment and affection; with wisdom, become capable of seeking Prabhu, take refuge in Paramatma only.

➤ What will happen by taking refuge...

☼ By doing so, becoming free of vanity and delusion, totally bereft of desires, free of pleasure-pain and duality, that human attains avinashi padd, the eternal imperishable state. The space which is not illumined by the sun moon or fire is my Param Dhaam, Supreme Abode.

- Attaining this eternal state, the human does not come back to this world, symbolising that the world no longer bothers him. But mistakenly, the human assumes the deeds of nature, senses and the mind to be his own. Due to this he gets caught in the cycle of birth and death. The wise one who has the eye of wisdom knows this secret that even while enjoying luxuries, the true state of the soul stays unaffected. The eye of wisdom opens only in an individual who has cleansed and purified his Inner-Self.

»➤ What is that tattve which is fixed in itself...

☀ I alone am in all... the effulgence of the sun moon and fire

- I am in all hearts
- I am the knower of all the Veds
- The Uttam Purush, ultimate human; kshar–akshar, mortal-immortal; vinashi-avinashi, perishable-imperishable, I am all.
- I am Purushottam, the superb human.

✳ *This is the truth, to be a superb human is to be Divine Being.*

BEING OF LIGHT.

|| ॐ ||

Superb Divine Human

There are six attributes of Prabhuta, THAT Greatness —

- *Poorn gyan — absolute knowledge of Para and Apara sciences.*

  Apara gyan is the acquired worldly knowledge, which can be defined by technology and science — factual knowledge.

  Para gyan is the knowledge of all that is beyond the mind. It is the knowledge of the Universe, of unseen worlds, dreams, coincidences and para-normal experiences that science cannot fathom. It is the revelation of the powers of the mind, its flights and fancies, invisible supernatural powers, inscrutable ways of the cosmic forces and all other fields which are beyond the realm of science as known today. These are guided by a supreme arrangement.

  Only the one who knows both Para and Apara sciences in totality can explain the para gyan based on apara gyan.

- *Poorn vairagya — Absolute renunciation from thoughts desires emotions people and environment for the expansion of the soul. Detachment that attaches with the entire universe equally. Detachment that is not indifference...*

- *Poorn dharm — Perfect conduct, every moment doing the right thing at the right time according to the need of that moment. Using all physical mental and spiritual capacities to the maximum, in accordance with laws of Nature.*
- *Poorn shobha — Complete grace, elegance in speech, deed and movement. Every gesture and act is full of poise. This is the manifestation of the ever-flowing grace arising and flowing from the Divine Consciousness within.*
- *Poorn aishwarya — Absolute opulence, abundance of everything, happiness joy peace solitude and compassion. Such a person has something joyous for everyone besides being an unlimited source of energy for others. New every time, all the time.*
- *Poorn yash — Absolute glory. Those who have imbibed the divine attributes have a completely positive aura at all times. Every thought word and deed is for universal benefit. Their aura continuously exudes rays of ever-increasing glory. There is no negativity from any direction.*

When totally replete with all the above six qualities four more are required to attain the Supreme Self.

These are: sacrifice, unconditional love, wisdom and acceptance.

When these divine qualities adorn a realised human, only then emerges a Bhagwat Swaroop, divine form whose mere sight is peaceful, whose every deed is attractive and sweet, speech has oaj, force of truth, and whose presence has a adviteeye tej, unique luminosity.

Pranam's pranam to all who are able to recognise such a wondrous luminous and soul-attracting being.

|| ॐ ||

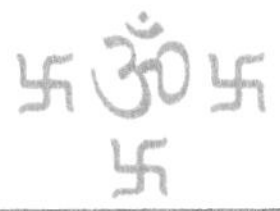

Om Parmatmaney Namah

Shree Krishnam Vande Jagadgurum

Jai Yogeshwar

Wednesday, 7.7.1993   Time: Night 10.12

Om Bram Breem Brom Seh Buddhaye Namah

Chapter 16

Divine and Demonic Attributes

➤ Prabho, who deserves to know the rarest of rare secrets of human and Brahm...

☀ The one who has divine attributes...

Divine attributes are liberating. Aasuri, demonic nature binds and is torturous like hell. People with aasuri tendencies do not have the awareness or wisdom to know what is to be denounced, what is to be favoured.

- They are not pure inside and outside...
- Devoid of good conduct, truth and contrarian views
- No faith in dharm and scriptures, know them to be false
- Do not believe in the existence of the soul or know it

- Insolent behaviour, enemies of the world
- Intoxicated with arrogance and pride of having the capacity to destroy others
- Roaming in the world, following impure niyam, rules, with misconceived zeal.

Whatever there is, it is here, sukh, bhog and sangreh, happiness, luxuries and collections, this is the thought. This much wealth is here and how to acquire more — only this is the aim. 'We are self-sufficient and powerful; we have killed many enemies and will suppress others too. We are wealthy, we can get anything. There is no one like us. We will do lots of charity and yagyas, rituals and enjoy.'

Because even their good deeds are an outcome of arrogance, they constantly keep an eye on the wealth and bad qualities of others.

Lust greed and anger are reasons for one's downfall... renounce these. Deeds sanctioned by scriptures are karm and duty.

A selfish karm performed according to mind games is akartavya-akarm, neither true duty nor true karm.

»➤ What are the characteristics of a human with such divine qualities...

☀ Taking refuge in me alone and being fearless...

- A single-minded resolve to attain me

- Maintaining equanimity in every situation so as to know me by my tattve, essence
- Giving charity with purity without any expectations
- Keeping senses under control
- Fulfilling all duties wholeheartedly
- Leading life according to scriptures
- Happily bearing the difficulties that come in the process of conducting human dharm
- Simplicity of the body mind and speech and not giving even the slightest pain to anyone through these
- Knowing all to be my forms, not getting angry at anyone
- Anything that is seen heard or understood, repeating it exactly the way as it is, in sweet words
- Renouncing worldly desires but not karm
- Not being restless within due to raag-dvesh, infatuation-resentment
- Not attached to worldly subjects
- Not gossiping
- Having compassion and being without greed
- Having tej, strength in the body, and oaj, power of truth in the speech

- No bhav of superiority
- No chapalta, fickleness; no fidgetiness
- Following the dharm of cleanliness of the body
- Being serene in every situation, always

- No feeling of vengeance
- Forgiving the misdeeds of the offender despite having the power to punish.

This is internal penance. By attempting to internalise these divine attributes, immense peace and wisdom are ignited, which help in performing acts of universal welfare that destroy the effects of aasuri qualities.

Awaken Now

Pranam awakens you
Know the sign of the Consciousness of the Age
Leave the slavery of the fickle mind
Recognise the truth of the inner consciousness
O Human!
The wheel of time has turned, time is changing, all
evolved souls are feeling emptiness and a strange
kind of stagnancy.

Open the locks of your heart, let the soul fly free like a bird. Accept your individual truths. Free yourself from dualities and suspicions. You will change. O Human, you will have to change. This is the only thing to know and understand that the time for change has arrived. Whether you like it or not, your mentality will get attracted to the truth because it is only you who has been searching for the truth since ages. Now it is time to live the truth else diseases depression agonies... knocks of destiny will torture you.

Use your dhyan and knowledge to understand all that is happening around you and flow with the call of time. Nothing is meaningless or without a reason. All are sources of inspiration to act according to the time so that you cannot say that you were not warned and you missed the message. Understanding the need and demand of time and deciding what is to be the karm accordingly will make you ascend that ladder of divinity which takes one to the pinnacle of human evolution.

By imbibing the divine wealth-laden qualities of the Geeta, divine attributes too get ignited.

|| ॐ ||

May Divine Qualities be the Gifts of Life

There are eighty-four lakh species in the world according to shastras and each one has its own nature and qualities provided by Nature.

The human is the only superb creation of Nature who has within him all of these bhav and qualities and lives them within his lifespan according to situations.

So heaven or hell is here itself. Those who live by incorporating the good qualities of Nature, the same become the reason for their genetic qualities. Thus, there is a constant incremental evolution of human potential.

The human can evolve his capacities to the extent that he becomes Bhagwat-swaroop, a reflection of the Divine, because the meaning of Bhagwan, Prabhu, is being superb ultimate perfection.

Whenever the mechanism of the world is disturbed and the importance of righteousness is devalued, then some thoughtful progressive absolute human arises and gets active to show the right path to the world.

To be worthy of human dharm and dharm of the Yug, work on oneself by perfecting and transforming these ten bhavs, feels —

- *Fear into love by realising that the same noor, divine effulgence, lies in all*
- *Acquired persona, hypocrisy, exhibitionist tendencies into Self-realisation and truth. There is no greater falsehood and hypocrisy than acquired image or an exhibitionistic personality*
- *Unnecessary pressure and control over others into karm and faith. Doing your designated task with full faith and trust is what inspires others*
- *Convert self-hatred and self-pity into 'self-strength' by gaining victory over them through awareness and dhyan*
- *Scientific knowledge and mind power into vidya and gyan, true education and true wisdom that become the rationale to act according to the time requirement*
- *Independence and self-sufficiency into forces complementing each other. To consider others inferior is a hindrance to evolution*
- *Vengeance and 'one-upmanship' into anand. Vengefulness leads to depression*
- *Anger into Durga Shakti, power to eradicate imperfection and falsehood*
- *Problems into surrender and true karm. Wisdom lies in accepting that life is like an examination paper*

- *Paucity of love into spreading of divine unconditional love; whatever you did not get, offer that generously to all.*

If you want others to agree with you then have faith in yourself. Stop worrying about what others think of you, just be honest to yourself. In the blind competitive rat race, the human has forgotten his special unique individuality. But now time has come to connect to the true source and roots that nourish his true dharm, to enable him to do justice to his existence.

|| ॐ ||

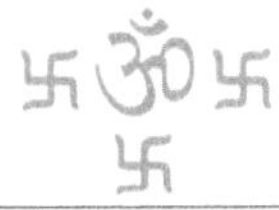

Om Parmatmaney Namah
Shree Krishnam Vande Jagadgurum
Jai Yogeshwar

Wednesday, 14.7.1993   Time: Night 1.05
Om Bram Breem Brom Seh Buddhaye Namah

Chapter 17

Three Kinds of Faith

»➤ How many kinds of shraddha, faith, are there and how to identify them...

✷ According to the human's natural tendency, faith can be rajasic tamasic or sattvic. Faith is according to ones antahkaran, Inner-Self. The sattvic worship devi-devtas; the rajasic worship yakshas and rakshas; while the tamasic worship ghosts and supernatural beings.

»➤ How to recognise those who do not worship or do any penance...

✷ Recognise them from their interest in food...

- The food of a sattvic person is that which imparts strength health peace and happiness, increases the life span, stability, provides strength to the heart, is full of rasa, like pure ghee, and is natural and seasonal

- The food of a rajasic person is smooth bitter sour salty hot pungent dry, roasted full of spices and that which is the cause of agony disease and grief
- The food of a tamasic person is semi-cooked or over-cooked stale without any rasa, over roasted and includes alcohol onion garlic meat. It induces aasuri attributes.

➤ How many forms of yagya are there...

✴ Yagya; daan, charity; and tap, penance; are of three kinds too

- Sattvic yagya is a duty karm, knowing this, it is to be performed without a desire for results
- Rajasic yagya is done for display or for selfish motives
- Tamasic yagya is conducted without faith, merely to harm others and show authority.

➤ How many types of tap are there, Prabho...

✴ Tap is of three kinds, the sattvic tap of body mind and speech is:

- Following great souls; leading a simple uncomplicated life; no arrogance; keeping the body pure through water and mud, natural products; causing no harm to anyone through the physical being — is bodily penance

- Udvaigheen vachan, dispassionate statements; truthful pleasant well-meaning words; self-study; practise; naam jap, chanting the name of Prabhu — is penance of the speech
- Inner happiness, gentle nature, introspective, having control over the mind and the purity of bhav, is the penance of the mind. These three kinds of sattvic tap of the body mind and speech, make one desireless.

»➤ What are rajasic and tamasic tap...

✺ Rajasic tap — the penance that is performed for self-glorification, self-worship and for the purpose of public display, has uncertain and perishable results.

Tamasic tap is performed out of sheer foolishness and stubbornness only to inflict discomfort on oneself and to torture others.

»➤ What are the three forms of daan...

✺ Doing charity is a duty. Charity that is done according to place and time and for the deserving ones, without seeking any returns is sattvic daan.

- Charity done for some results is rajasic

- Giving without reverence, with contempt, to the undeserving is tamasic
- The one who does not have the knowledge of the true dharm, for him chanting the mantra Hariom Tatt Satt before every task and remembering Paramatma is enough to sanctify it.

Om — the first uttered word, the imperishable

Tatt — everything belongs to THAT

Satt — all the karm performed for that Prabhu is 'satt', true, pure

- Without wisdom and faith, all jap and tap are futile, mere hypocrisy. These cannot bear satt results.

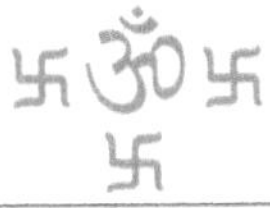

Om Parmatmaney Namah
Shree Krishnam Vande Jagadgurum
Jai Yogeshwar

Wednesday, 4.8.1993   Time: Night 10:21

Om Bram Breem Brom Seh Buddhaye Namah

Chapter 18

Yog of Deliverance and Renunciation

»➤ O Antaryami, knower of every mind, what is the difference between tyag and sanyas; sacrifice and renunciation...

☀ There are four different views about sacrifice and renunciation:

- Sanyas is renunciation of all acts arising from kamyakarm, worldly cravings
- Tyag is total renunciation of fruits of all actions
- Wisdom lies in removing like a dosha, flaw, the karta bhav, sense of 'doership', from all actions
- Gyan tap jap are not to be renounced
- Dropping all pining for the fruit of karm, doing karm according to dharm, performing all kartvaya karm, duty karm, is the best.

Avoiding duty karm due to indulgence arising from attachment or greed is tamas. Feeling harassed and complaining about duty-bound actions is rajas. Doing kartvaya karm without expecting results, devoid of distress is sattvic. Renounce the desire for the fruit of karm, not the karm itself. The karm is to be performed without attachment and desire for the fruit of action. A viveki tyagi, wise renouncer, is centred in himself without any doubts and dualities.

»➤ Why so much botheration, why not renounce actions altogether...

⚛ The one who has a body cannot renounce action
Only the desire for results is to be renounced.
Three kinds of fruits of karm are:
- Ishtt, circumstances or situations that a human wants
- Anishtt, situations the human does not want
- Mishr, results that are a mix of ishtt and anishtt.

»➤ For karm, who is the kaaran, reason, and the madhyam, medium...

⚛ Shareer — body
- Karta — doer

- Vividh kaaran — multiple causes
- Bhin bhin cheshtayien — different kinds of efforts
- Sanskars — inherent values.

✳ *'I am the doer,' this is an arrogant bhav; the one who performs karm without this bhav is never bound by his karm.*

➤ If actions do not have any relation to the soul, then under whose prerna, inspiration, does karm happen...

☀ Karm is inspired by gyan — acquired knowledge; gyey, that which is imbibed; and parigyata, the knower or one who understands this gyan.
Kaaran — reason
Indriyan — senses
Karta — doer
Karm — action, these are the reasons for the accumulation of karm.

✳ *Karm creates karma and only karm can cut karma, if done with the whole being, as arpan, offering to Prabhu. (Karm—action, Karma—result of cause & effect)*

☀ In this world, the classification into Brahmin Kshatriya Vaishya and Shudra has been done on the basis of gunas that have emerged from human nature. Hence, doing designated duty as ordained by the varna, caste, is the only solution to mitigate gunas.

Swabhavik karm, natural karm; varna vibhajan, caste classification is based on the inherent tendencies of the individual.

Brahmin Karm:

Restraining the mann, mind, heart

- Controlling the senses
- Bearing the troubles on the path of dharm
- Being pure outside and inside
- Forgiving others' misdeeds
- Simplicity of the body mind and heart
- Reiteration of the gyan of the Veds, shastras
- Practising and experiencing the process of yagya
- Having faith in Paramatma, Veds.

Kshatriya Karm:

- Being brave and courageous
- Effulgent
- Being tolerant
- Having organisational skills
- Not turning back on strife or war
- Doing charity
- Ruling.

Vaishya Karm:

- Agriculture, agrarian profession and nurturing cows...
- Honest, clean business, managing society's economy.

Shudra Karm:

- Serving all the four varnas.

The human who performs the karm of his varna as per his natural instinct, based on his natural nature, dutifully and without any attachment merges in Paramatma, Supreme Soul.

✷ *This classification is according to karm and not any caste. Every type of human can do work according to his capacities and capabilities, supporting each other for harmonious co-existence.*

»➤ How to attain Paramatma...

☀ Hear from me and reflect — by performing karm like worship the human attains siddhis, special accomplishments, or proficiencies. He attains Param + Atma = Paramatma, becomes THAT. By performing actions as his ordained nature, natural nature and swadharma swaroop, according to his own dharm, the human does not become party to sin.

Even if it is flawed, own dharm should not be relinquished.

- Just like when a fire is lit, it first gives off smoke, similarly at the beginning of each karm, there is bound to be some flaw or the other.

➤ Prabho... so as to not bear even the slightest flaw in karm, what is the solution...

✴ Sankhya yog — an intellect sans attachment; with control over the body; not even slightly concerned about any object, such a person attains naishkarmye siddhi — absolute detachment from karmphal.

➤ Prabho... what is the kram, sequence, to attain naishkarmye siddhi...

✴ For the human to attain the ultimate gyan that will help him perfect the purity of the Inner-Self leading to the attainment of Brahm, the kram is thus:

- Have sattvic, pure intellect
- Take refuge in detachment
- Be solitary by nature
- Have proper eating habits
- Manage senses with patience
- Have control over body mind and speech
- Renounce subjects of lust in words and thoughts

- Renounce rage and resentment
- Constantly remember Paramatma.

A human who has renounced pride stubbornness arrogance lust anger, and parigraha, hoarding, without the bhav of mine and thine, becomes peaceful and is worthy of attaining the Brahm.

»➤ Prabho... what happens by becoming worthy...

☀ That sadhak upon attaining the Brahm-bhoot awastha, the state of knowing, realising Brahm, is always joyful, neither grieves for anyone nor desires anything. His whole being is in sambhaav, same with all creatures. Such a person attains my para-bhakti, supreme devotion.

»➤ What after attaining para-bhakti, Prabho...

☀ In that para-bhakti one knows: 'Whatever I am, however I am, I am yours'. Knowing me thus by the essence he immediately merges in me. The best means to attain me is taking refuge in me with ananya bhav, unflinching feel.

»➤ What should I do...

☀ Just be absorbed in me in entirety and offer all actions to me. Remove the feeling of belonging, 'my-ness' from all actions and objects...

- Attain equanimity and 'merey mann wala ho jaa' — be of my mann, heart and soul.

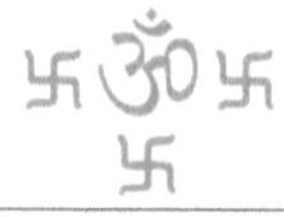

Through this, due to my benevolence you shall sail through all hurdles and troubles.

Being egoistic, if you don't follow this, there will be denouement.

»➤ How will this lead to downfall, Prabho...

☀ Making a decision not to go to war by taking refuge in ego and attachment is being untruthful.

Because your kshaatr prakriti, nature of a warrior, will make you go to war.
The Antaryami Eeshwar, omniscient Prabhu, makes all who have been blessed with the body as an instrument, wander in this world through his maya, based on their natural inherent nature, caste by birth.

- Call it whatever — Chetan tattve, the conscious element
- Pragyanam Brahm — the Brahm that lies beyond the mind.
  Because the human works according to his nature, which is a product of heredity, nature bestowed by Nature and sanskars inherited by birth backed by inspiration from the Inner-Self.

»➤ What is the remedy to come out of this subjugation...

With absolutely sincere devotion, take refuge in the Antaryami Eeshwar, the All-knowing Supreme.

Be in poorn samarpan, whole and complete surrender.

By His divine grace, due to absolute disenchantment from the world, the indestructible state will be attained.

Now you think contemplate absolutely, do as you feel; listen to the voice of the soul.

I can't think, tell me what to do, Prabho…

Be of my mann; mujhe hee pranam kar, bow to me alone. Leave dependency on all worldly religions; take refuge in me.

I will liberate you from all sins.

You have shared a very good nice and easy solution, may I share it with others… Prabho…

No, no, no Bhaiya, my dear, do not share it with the one who is intolerant, not my devotee, finds fault in me and certainly does not want to hear about me.

Whom should I tell…

To my devotees, the humans with the aim of parabhakti, ultimate devotion, who will further share this supreme secret with other devotees.

- Such a person without doubt shall attain me
- He will be extremely dear to me
- Whoever merely studies this dharm samvaad, conversation about dharm, will worship me through his gyan yagya
- Even those who listen to it with great reverence will be delivered from all sins.

Parth, now I have one question. Has your moh, infatuation, stemming from ignorance been destroyed...

Listening to your discourse my moh has been eliminated and I have regained wisdom and smriti, memory. But this has happened because of your benevolence, not because of gyanopdesh, wise-discourse.

Now, without any duality I am equipoised
I will obey your directives.

With the benevolence of Ved Vyas, Maa Saraswati, I Sanjay, meena manu received this dialogue between Krishn and Arjun, straight from the mouth of Yogeshwar Shree Krishn, heard it and realised it and drank this amrit, nectar drop by drop to my heart's content.

How... why... did I receive this wisdom, why Supreme considered me supatr, deserving of this... that too in Kali yug... because my being is his ansh, particle; vansh, lineage; the only thing remaining was to realise this. This is true gyan..

Grateful just grateful... full of gratitude. My whole existence is brimming with gratitude, ecstatic again and again... enraptured...

Sanjay:

Yatr Yogeshwar Krishno Yatr Partho
Dhanurdharah
Tattr Shreevijayo Bhutirdhruva
Neetirmatirmamah.

Wherever there is Krishn, the master of every yog, and wherever there is Arjun, the supreme archer, there will also be abundance glory victory good senses and right conduct for sure.

This is my opinion.

Divine Ecstasy

Meena is established in supreme bliss
I am an ansh, a minute particle of that Viraat
Swaroop, enormous form
Thinking again and again about it
My weightless heart, floating like
a flower in the air
Is engrossed
Immersed in Prabhu
Wherever there is Shree Krishn the Jagadguru
Arjun determinded, capable of targeting
the goal is there
There lies shree, glory
There lies vijay, victory
There is vibhuti, grandeur and
unflinching righteousness
Pranav, Om
Pratyaksh, visible
Praman, evident
Pranam: expansion of the soul with humility
Path: Truth Love Karm and Light

This is Truth
Truth is here.

|| ॐ ||

Insights into Krishn Consciousness

ॐ

Om - the Sound Projection
of Supreme Entity

Om is the Dhwani Murti, sound manifestation,
Expression of the sound vibration of Supreme.
Om is the word representation of Param Brahm.
Setting aside even the word form eventually
And by going beyond...
The subtlest is to be realised.
This is Nitya Geeta.

First, the subtle body is to be reached through
atma-anubhuti, soul realisation.
Then the subtler cosmic body is to be known.
Knowing its gyan vigyan, knowledge and science,
then realising the param-tattve, the subtlest
supreme essence...
Eventually merging with it
For Ekattva-anubhuti, feeling of Oneness.

The one who has come to feel and realise that anhad naad, the unstruck cosmic sound, and has internalised the vibrations of its experience, whatever he utters that becomes Ved, Upanishad, Geeta. This resonance is in everyone's niyati, destiny, because within all is the vibration that empowers the life force. But to experience and feel it, the first step is the absolute renunciation of noisy meaningless indecent and ugly words. Be truthful and same on all three planes, thought word and deed.

That is why Shree Krishn states in the Geeta — 'nirantar Om japo aur mera dhyan dharo', do constant jap of Om and put dhyan on MY BEING.

This is Truth
Truth is here.

Jai Satyeshwar

|| ॐ ||

The Essence of Wisdom

After practising the knowledge imparted by the scriptures for real insights, the medhavi, brilliant one, should then shed the mass of bookish knowledge just as chaff is discarded after sifting the grains.

Like butter hidden in milk, true deep knowledge and science dwell in the Inner-Self of all beings. With the mind as a churning rod, whisk it out with absolute attention and constant dhyan, contemplation.

Minimising bodily needs and contracting outer expansions, travel on an inner journey. 'Jahan jaaye dhyan wahin bane Bhagwan', To whatever one applies dhyan, attention, that becomes one's Bhagwan.

As is Bhagwan, same will be the gunas, accordingly will be the karm, the result too will be in consonance with that.

|| ॐ ||

Realisation

My being is knowing and realising the Truth. Being a link in the chain of the lineage of Avtar Consciousness, the same consciousness that directs Avtars by becoming the voice of their conscience is also directing me.

An Avtar always seeks blessings of gurus because he can never forget even for a second that he is human and has to be perfect in his human-to-human conduct also. It is his natural nature and inclination to respect and serve his elders, the learned, evolved souls and guru-swamis. To be constantly aware of abiding by these sanskars, values, always is the pinnacle of humility of an Avtar.

Shree Krishn always touched the feet of all the elders, from grandfather Bheeshm to aunt Kunti, with complete respect. He obtained the blessings of all gurus, from rishis Sandipani to Kripacharya, Dronacharya, to the extent that at the time of the Mahabharat, during the ceasefire at night, he would visit everybody's camp casually, completely maintaining worldly conduct. Shree Ram also fully served obeyed and emulated the instructions of gurus. He was always hesitant even to have his feet touched. He only conceded because of the love-soaked words of Kevat, the boatman, and the innocent heart-touching persistence of others.

Shree Krishn, the master of yog, became a charioteer, alone unarmed without any guard or other security arrangements. He himself became the armour of his friend Arjun for the sake of pure love.

On the other side, Duryodhan organised a huge protective ring and shield of brave warriors for Bheeshm. All the gurus knew that Krishn was an Avtar, even then who listened to him... Neither to his earlier offer of truce, nor to the ethical eternally wise words of the Geeta. All of them were busy justifying their deeds according to their gyan, they continued to do so till the very end. But eventually, while lying on a bed of arrows at the time of his death even Bheeshm Pitamah expected deliverance from Shree Krishn.

The reality is that because the Avtar lives amongst them with complete humility like a human and serves everyone by winning their hearts and keeping them happy, everyone has expectations of him. But there are only a few who follow his truthful utterances and act accordingly. Very few can understand the pain of an Avtar. Everyone tastes and experiences his beautiful energetic illuminated and fragrant aura. The absolutely wonderful pleasant environment that is experienced in the company of an Avtar is taken for granted.

An Avtar is an eternal vagabond. With a heart full of love, keeping the pangs of separation to himself, without getting aggrieved, becoming an embodiment of detachment and absolute karm, he keeps on changing his circle, helping people wherever he goes to mitigate their karmas. When did any Avtar ever deliver sermons gathering a huge crowd... Whatever he lives, experiences, learns from life and realises through contemplation according to time requirement, when expressed, becomes the Geeta.

The seventh Avtar, Shree Ram, would often become teary-eyed and express separation longing compassion gratitude and love. The eighth Avtar, Shree Krishn, solah kala sampoorn, master of sixteen arts, would conceal his tears, never let them show and always flashed that enchanting smile.

Very rarely does someone become a co-traveller and confidante of an Avtar. People listen to guru-swamis, try to follow and worship them while they are alive, but an Avtar is adored and worshipped after his exit. They try to understand his or her conduct and statements but cannot fathom them completely. They can only describe them in their own way through lectures, detailed explanations, in this the real truth gets lost and trying to understand this truth, the yug changes. Then, according to the new Age and Time, Yug and Kaal, time to add something new to that truth arrives. The one who adds this new gyan again goes unrecognised because the search for past images still persists. The real truth gets lost in the newly prevalent ritualistic ways of devotion, new temples, various types of presentations and prayer meetings. This is the irony of the paradigmatic exemplary truthful one. Who understands him in his lifetime...

So the point to be realised is that by not understanding and just listening to mythological tales nothing can be accomplished as revealed, lived and stated by Avtars. They showed and chalked out the path by being an example. Now it is the turn to be aware and act according to the Geeta. The capacity and endeavour to realise this has certainly been bestowed upon all by Supreme and Nature.

This is Truth
Truth is here.

|| ॐ ||

Identification of an Avtar

Part 1

These days there is an abundance of knowledge. Everyone is playing according to their guna or qualities and eulogising only that. But the truth is that to recognise the viraat roop or colossal form of an Avtar, a nidrajayee, an awakened one having true wisdom, an eager enquirer like Arjun is needed.

An Avtar is the ultimate culmination of human evolution. There are seven stages of evolution of the jeev, sentient being:

- Animal
- Human
- Devta
- Saint, Seer
- Guru, Acharya
- Paramhans
- Avtar or the complete manifestation of Nature.

The animal stage is the aadhaar, base for energy to move upwards for growth and human evolution starts from this point, for example, Matasya, Kurmi, Varah, Narsimh, Vaman, Parashuram, Ram, Krishn, Buddh and Kalki.

Being a human is the highest on the scale of evolution, yet it carries the gunas, attributes or reflections of eighty-four lakh species. To become a devta, humans have to refine and purify these gunas or attributes. The devta state has happiness, opulence and the ability to help others but it is fraught with the constant fear of losing power and wealth. The state of the saint is free from such fears; there is perpetual bliss and solitude. Guru acharya paramhans, seated in high positions, guide the human towards evolution with their intelligence and knowledge. They know the attributes of 'Avtarhood', but they are not that.

An Avtar is an example of the ultimate human being of the era. It is the most evolved blissful state, sachchidanand — state of perpetual anand of truthful chitt, to show the path of enlightenment to humanity. This state is silently and effortlessly prepared by Nature's Supreme Intelligence to deliver human beings from their self-created cobwebs and labyrinths of life.

An Avtar has no title or aasan, pedestal. He seems to belong to all. 'O Ram! Where are you...' 'Where have you been, Gopal...' This is how people address them, not as 'Shri Shri 108 acharya swami mahamahim paramhans etc.'

That is why Shree Krishn stated in the Geeta: The ignorant ones think of me as a regular human being living among them. Do not tell or reveal my marm, secret, to those who do not have faith in me. But one thing is for sure, be assured that whenever there are inquirers like Arjun, Krishn will not be far behind. This is sambhavami yuge yuge — an assurance of the descent of an Avtar in every Age, Yug. Whenever humanity's questions reach their peak then according to the need of that Yug an evolved soul is always there to answer.

All spoken and written words are truth of the moment they have been uttered or written but by the time people start relating to them, time has already moved on. Similarly, people look for a replica or reflection of that previous Avtar, whereas the truth is that no two Avtars are similar, their form and role change according to the requirement of the time.

This is Truth
Truth is here.

|| ꣐ ||

Identification of an Avtar

Part 2

An Avtar has only one aim: To establish the continuance of Truth Love Karm and Light, by being a perfect paradigm. 'Avtar' is derived from the word 'avataran,' descent.

An Avtar, renouncing the glory and pride of his supreme status, performs leelas, worldly plays, like an ordinary human to allure humans to show them the Way. His only dharm is karm, duty-action, to work constantly to remove imperfection and ignorance, living amidst all the vicissitudes of life.

Every evolved human belongs to a chain. Based on his capacity and distinct individuality, the human connects to a particular chain. A saint to a saint, mahatma to a mahatma... This is Nature's law. An Avtar naturally appears in the consciousness of an Avtar and delivers complete instructions about what he needs to do in future — 'now you manage the future karm, and according to time requirement, you will have to add something new in a new way.' He sows the sankalp, makes a pledge according to what has to be done in the future.

A yogi to a yogi and an acharya to an acharya, effortlessly pass on their status and directives as secret to others.

But an Avtar is chosen absolutely by Nature. Nature through its own special tests according to time, bestows perfection on the Avtar. Due to this direct connection with Nature, the messages of evolution are manifested through the Avtar and transmitted to further yugs and thus, Nature continues to evolve uttrottar, progressively.

Remembering everything since the creation of Creation and understanding all secrets and truths is Manusmriti, perpetual memory. Even in the Geeta, Shree Krishn says that Manu came to know of all the truth and facts from Suryadev, the Sun. Slowly this knowledge got lost but Arjun received it once again in the form of the Geeta.

The truth of the Veds; facts of science; gyan va vivek, knowledge and wisdom; and vidya va shiksha, education and learning; when the human perfects all these four planes, they become his natural nature and keep flowing spontaneously from his being. What is thought, is lived, is said and put into action.

Everything happens by being one on the three planes of mansa vacha karmana, mind speech and deed. His entire human yantra, tantra and mantra, machine, mechanism and the corresponding sound vibration, become a manifestation of the Brahmandiye Bodhi, Universal Intelligence, which is eternally orchestrating this world by being a witness, detached and unaffected. And for this, it does not need any external force. Everything happens spontaneously and effortlessly through atma-shakti, soul-power.

This is Truth
Truth is here.

|| ॐ ||

Avtar is Supreme Divinity

A unique quality of Avtars is that the people who associate with them also become famous, immortal. Along with Shree Krishn, his friends Arjun, Sudama and Radha... with Shree Ram, Sita and Hanuman too are revered and remembered. In Kaliyug, the Avtar manifests the force of Truth. The sword of Truth cuts all ignorance and imperfections that have crept into the process of human evolution.

The weapons used by Avtars of the four Yugs are:
1. Satyug is Shiv Yug, the hathiyar, weapon, is dhyan.
2. Tretayug is Ram Yug, the weapon is dhanush baan, bow and arrow, empowered by dhyan.
3. Dwaparyug is Krishn Yug, the weapon is Sudarshan Chakra, satya ka darshan, used to eliminate adharm with dhyan.
4. In Kaliyug, satya ki talwar, sword of truth, is the weapon and work is accomplished by the most evolved consciousness of the Age, connected to Krishn Consciousness, backed by the force of dhyan.

In every Yug, dhyan is to be realised and perfected, supported by pure Consciousness, to get things done according to Param Chetna, Supreme Intelligence.

An Avtar is the most evolved human who realises the time requirement of that Age, Sambhavami Yuge Yuge, and manifests whenever Nature's creations are in acute turmoil.

Shree Vishnu, the preserver, resurrector and reformer, takes Avtar and keeps reappearing in consequent forms, according to the need of the time, to re-establish the true Sanatan Dharm, shaswat satya sanatan vastvik dharm, eternal true perpetual real dharm, for the sake of humanity.

The Avtar knows well who is at what stage of evolution.

To continue evolving in proper and true direction, two things are required: absolute surrender and unflinching bhakti — love and faith.

|| ॐ ||

Realisation of True Gyan is
Sudarshan Chakra of Pranam

A lot has been conveyed through signs, poems and the hide-and-seek of language. Full effort has been made to awaken the human from slumber to become an Arjun, know satya-dharm, true conduct and ascertain his path. Just as the warning 'run for cover' is given before an attack, the message of Time is to be conveyed so as to provide some relief to human from the fire initiation that Nature has in store for his falsehood and imperfections. Nature too takes the form of Shiv and performs the tandav or the dance of destruction; Nature starts giving messages in sign language and also prepares some humans to perceive those signs or messages and warn humanity.

Pranam is one such medium, which is in constant connection with Nature and its laws of Kalchakra, Time Wheel, which knows the truth that the rise in falsehood and imperfection is an indication that poornta, absoluteness, and truth are also close by. Like Arjun, whenever a human, hardworking and wise, is at the crossroads and anxious, Krishn is not far away. Divine vision of wisdom is required to see Krishn's viraat roop, celestial cosmic form, absolute surrender is required to feel it and get empowered to do karm accordingly. A creation of Time, Krishn is ever ready to become the charioteer of every willing Arjun.

Pranam has repeatedly stated that now everyone will have to go through fire-initiation, internal fires and external fires. External fires include earthquakes wars accidents bombs fires etc and internal fires are diseases that even science will not be able to diagnose and cure. This message was conveyed to everyone in the year 1999 on the day of Guru Purnima.

A few sensitive people get drawn to the Truth, they support and strengthen faith in the Truth to resurrect the path of human towards transformation and growth. What a paradox it is that falsehood unites with falsehood instantly and keeping one-point programme in mind, fulfils its evil designs but truth is never willing to join hands with truth.

Now the time has come when falsehood will kill falsehood. Those who adopt the truth and take shelter in divine qualities and walk on the right path as directed in the Geeta, without any doubt, will resurrect the path to Satyug. Truth will conquer because after Kaliyug, Satyug is sure to come. Human has to return to the primordial shashwat Sanatan Dharm, eternal constant dharm, Ved Dharm that manifested on Earth. In between on the path of human evolution, the religions that came up were the result of time requirement but the selfish human mind distorted them.

Now anything with contamination, whether it is religious social political or individual, will have to go through fire initiation. All will have to stand in the witness box in the court of Truth. It is the destiny of falsehood and imperfection to get destroyed.

Kalki Avtar will deliver the world. His sword symbolises wisdom and his horse means power reaching all directions. After maha-vinash, mass destruction, fire initiation, the feeling of Vasudhaiv Kutumbkum, that the whole world is a family, will prevail. This Avtar may be in the form of a human, an organisation, collective, a force of consciousness or a line of thought but one thing is certain, some chosen medium will become a reason for its manifestation.

This is Truth
Truth is here.

Where is the 'I' Now...

When awakened
One goes beyond the karm
That is performed
For the need to hoard
For the sake of some gains...
When beyond it
One starts evolving
And becomes more sensitive towards love
Feels the love bestowed by others
And along with it
Arises an unbridled aspiration
To spread and flow
Expand the love...
Love becomes your existence
You become love that you are
Now no 'I' remains

This is Truth
Truth is here.

|| ॐ ||

My Supreme, Eeshwar

O human!

My Eeshwar is Truth. Like space air fire water and earth, alive and gatimaan, always on the move like Nature. The Eeshwar that acharyas gurus swamis and knowledgeable souls are scared of, make others fearful of, is not the Supreme Providence. THAT is eternal, without beginning or end, source and base of the entire creation. Arguments just negate and give rise to negativity.

> My being — reflection of Supreme Will
> Param satya — Supreme Truth
> Param prem — Supreme Love
> Param karm — Supreme Action
> Param prakash — Supreme Light.

The one who is the source of all these is my true constant consistent immortal Eeshwar, Supreme. You can manifest your own Supreme. Nature has bestowed each human with the ability of Eeshwar sakshaatkar, divine revelations, of the Supreme Entity. It maybe different from what I have realised, enshrined in my being. To reach your Eeshwar is to have firm faith in yourself. To retain and stay centred in it, sadhna of Truth is indispensible.

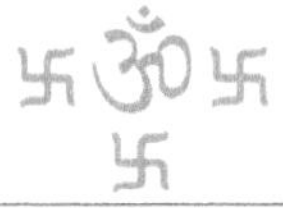

So O human! Do the penance of working on yourself. Know and understand the messages and directives of Supreme Consciousness and establish uchchtam adarsh, the highest of ideals. By having unflinching trust in yourself, create your own Eeshwar. Know and acknowledge the truth of existence and justify your human life. Supreme Truth can only be realised when you comprehend your truth.

Jai Satyeshwar

|| ॐ ||

Know the Truth

Thou are the Akshar Brahm, eternal eternity
Thou are the seed of the essence
Thou are the imperishable tattve, element
Thou are the vinashi, destructive tattve
Thou are the essence of the virtuous mind
Thou are the essence of the evil mind
Thou are the essence of Satan
Thou are the essence of Prabhu...

Human mind when in tune is Sur, divine
When out of tune is Asur, demon.

This is Truth
Truth is here.

|| ॐ ||

Supreme Provider

I turned to my creator for providence
I found my solace in Nature
And lo! Nature provided me with everything
Pampered all my emotional needs
Gave me energy for all worldly tasks and
sublime deeds
Quenched my thirst for knowledge
Pierced through the clouds of my suspicions
Dissolved all doubts and illusions on this earth
Queries related to my existence
And secrets of the universe
All were answered
It is then that I hugged
Pure Consciousness
Now we are inseparable co-travellers
Knowing each other
Feeling each other
Communicating in silence
Aware of the same thought at the same time
The feeling of the Soul
The thought which is not being thought
It is a beautiful happening
A miraculous splendid happening
No duality
No polarity
Perfect regularity...
I dwell now in the nucleus

The point of total merging
One mass of energy floating on all planes
of energy
Effortlessly surging with the essence
of the moment
O Nature! My love
It is so simple
I turned to you and you made me a
provider like you
Without any effort
But I am not a provider
I am in total surrender witnessing
The Supreme Providence
With complete gratitude.

This is Truth
Truth is here.

|| ॐ ||

Dissolving absolutely in the poorn, absolute
This is possible only through absolute surrender
Your existence, whole existence
Merging with only THAT Absolute
Is Param Yog, Supreme Merging.

|| ॐ ||

Song of the Soul

I am the consciousness of the Age
The words of the sage
The facts of the Ved
The confirmation science conveyed
The melody of the Geeta
The wisdom of the Geeta
The psychic daughter of Nature
The best creation of Nature
The mind of Time
To act according to Time
To the perfection of the moment
The manifestation of Truth
I am THAT
See the sun of the truth dawn
Behold the colours of the rainbow blown
Riding the chariot of seven horses
The wealth that truth endorses
Beyond the horizon
Deeper than deep
Where the human mind can't steep
To the core of forty-nine...All DIVINE
All Divine
Hear the rhyme of the Geeta ALIVE
Not incomprehensible
Simple and LIVE
With a medium beset with balance rhythm
and harmony

Why is life then an agony...
KRISHN CONSCIOUSNESS is here in full glory
The acclaim of wisdom
The flame of truth
The realm of Karm
To teach what life is about again and again
With the power of Para Force in this reign
Learn the way of life in right connection
Lead life with celebration
Attain perfection, discard imperfection
The union of universal forces
Solar and Lunar, Shiv and Shakti
Satyam Shivam Sunderam
In all, once again a perfect manifestation
To lead the revolution
Of human evolution.

This is Truth
Truth is here.

|| ॐ ||

Pranam is Proof

Of Truth
Of Love
Of Karm
Of Light
See by surrendering your whole being
Surrender is also possible only by Divine Grace
Aspire for this benevolence.

For Pranam, the truth is that
Which is realised through experience

All religious books and great scriptures Ved etc.
Are extremely knowledgeable
But without living their knowledge
Detailing it like mere gyan
Is the work of a storyteller or a discourser
Not the dharm of a truthful soul
The truthful soul states only that which has been
derived through living it
The utterances of the true soul are like mantras
Meaningless conversation is also falsehood.

Jai Satyeshwar

|| ॐ ||

Mana Marg of Pranam

Based on the directives of the Geeta
The four auspicious arms
Of Truth Love Karm and Light

Realise the eternity of universal laws of Truth Love Karm and Light. All are from one Supreme Source. Every happening on mental and physical planes creates ripples in the vast ocean of Universal Consciousness. Do the sadhna of sending waves of thoughts of satyam shivam sunderam, truth, welfare of all and beauty, for all in dhyan.

Love — you are human and humanity is your true religion based on laws of Nature. Be a provider protector preserver and destroyer of imperfections seeping into the infallible karma cycle.

Karm — you are the most perfect creation of Nature. Act like Nature, doing constant karm towards transformation and evolution. 'Duty karm' is dharm of life — duty karm of human towards the self, others, humanity, planet and the universe. Nothing that comes in the path of life is to be renounced, it is to be rejoiced by living every moment with your whole being.

Light — all are couriers of Supreme Light and delight. Negate all falsehood hypocrisy and ignorance and

be centred in Sachidanand, the joy of truthful chitt.
Supreme always propels humans towards the light of
Truth.

Truth Love Karm and Light for universal welfare
Make auspicious, the whole earth and sky
These four abodes are satyam shivam sunderam
Salutations to the luminous foursome.

Jai Satyeshwar

To have knowledge is good
To live according to it is better
But to be that is the best.

|| ॐ ||

Promise of Shree Krishn

The assurance of Shree Krishn
sambhavami yuge yuge —
Descent according to time
requirement in every Age...

The manifestation of Supreme Intelligence
manifested in visible form
Will happen
Always happens
Will continue to happen

These are not mere words
But a Truth — alive
A reality
A human who lives and dies for his vision,
After his body perishes
That vision will incarnate itself in thousand forms.

This is Truth
Truth is here.

|| ॐ ||

How to Study the Geeta

The Geeta is not merely a book. It is a mahamantra of how a human can become a super human by connecting with Supreme Consciousness. The Geeta is a guideline for working on the self silently, without setting aside any separate time for the internal sadhna for realising the reality of life and to become a part of constant evolution according to the laws of Nature.

The Geeta is for the realisation of the science of the cell carrying the universal consciousness in the body — how a cell relates to each and every other cell of the body with its own intelligence, for constantly eliminating undesirable elements which are a hindrance in growth and evolution because cells are programmed for making us a true human, part and parcel of Divinity.

Mind games and behaviour of the human, governed by jealousy resentment rage greed and attachment, instigate cells to behave in a manner which is against their true nature. So, all disharmonies — pains diseases sufferings accidents guilts and fears — surface to engage the mind in finding shortcuts to remove these by some techniques, suggestions, some ashirwaad or blessings from evolved souls.

The human does not think that he himself is the cause of all miseries because he has not recognised his true Self. For that one has to work on oneself constantly with dhyan. Only the Geeta states it with such clarity purity and wisdom that directly flows from the mouth of Shree Govind, Yogeshwar 'Satyeshwar', connected to Yug Chetna, Consciousness of the Age, and merged with Supreme essence, Param Tattve.

The title 'Shree Krishn' is the symbol of the highest evolved human of the Age, who descends to resurrect the true Sanatan Dharm as it is meant to be on the earth.

How to study contemplate and live the Geeta:

The Geeta is not meant to be read like a book, cover to cover. Whenever there is some doubt duality disturbance or question in the mind, close your eyes in absolute surrender and with complete reverence open the Geeta and ponder on the text that appears first. Just concentrate on that, learn the meaning of that and imbibe it.

Be your own judge, what is lacking or what has to be worked upon as sadhna, do it without having any doubts. Watch, observe after imbibing and working upon it, what questions or suspicions are arising. Just ponder and do chintan mannan, contemplate and meditate on that truthfully. After working on these points whatever question or doubt surfaces very clearly, open the Geeta again and just read the text that appears and do sadhna on it.

Keep reading studying and working on it like this. It may take time according to individual capacity and attributes. Never compare yourself with others. It is all about individual journey. The Geeta calls for absolute surrender and faith in the Divine Will.

The most important thing is to believe that what is being read in the Geeta is the voice of Supreme Consciousness. This is a learning on how to imbibe the truth without doubt and questioning.

Gradually, the Geeta will unfold all the secrets of human existence and full blossoming of divinity within, which will enable the sakshatkar, realisation of the Truth of Supreme Consciousness.

Living the Geeta is like a treasure hunt, one goes on collecting clues for further journey. Once the essence of the Geeta starts flowing and the urge to read it whole and complete arises from within, read it till the end again and again.

Along with the journey of life, the Geeta's form and meaning keep changing; new buds keep blooming.

To understand the Geeta and grow with it, it has to be lived, only then its deepest gyan starts to become comprehensible and descends in the life's Kurukshetra and begins to guide every moment. Only then the poorn astitva, whole existence, becomes Krishnamaye, immersed in Krishn Consciousness.

Pranam's heartfelt obeisance and thousands and thousands of salutations to the Geeta and the creator of the Geeta.

Pranam Om Om Om

Manasvini

Journey of the Nitya Geeta

Pranam!

Only through Supreme Divine grace this humble offering in the yagya of translation of the Nitya Geeta is being made... it is not me...it is not me...

My first introduction to the Geeta happened after meeting Meena Om ji in 1998, not because she mentioned and quoted the scripture but because of a vision of the viraat roop that happened to me one night soon after my introduction to her. I felt myself being extended and enhanced with Meena ji holding my hand, the voice in the background instructing 'manu viraat roop mein aao'...Manu take the form of viraat roop – the grandiose form of the Supreme. She grew bigger vaster and higher than all the mountains around breaking through space and extending into the infiniteness of the Universe, and I grew along with her.

Thereafter, my first copy, a commentary on the Geeta by Dr. S Radhakrishnan became an obsession. I would carry it everywhere, randomly opening its pages and aligning the questions in my being with the answers that the shloks offered.

Each and every translation from evolved ones has imparted greater insights into this marvellous scripture, but something always seemed incomplete until I read the Nitya Geeta. As I grew in Pranam, I understood that the Geeta is not just a scripture, it is a path that is alive in every Age to guide humanity towards Self-realisation and understanding the existence.

The Nitya Geeta manifested through the medium of Meena Om ji, and after years of its descent, she decided to compile it in its current form. Eager to know the most contemporary version coming directly from someone who actually lives every word of the Geeta, the impossible task of translating it into English was embarked upon.

The journey started somewhere in early 2014 while I was going through a particularly tough period at work and soon after initiating this task, a pattern emerged. A few verses or pages would be translated, never ever a full chapter, and then it would come to a grinding halt. My being would lose interest and would get sucked into the maze of worldly mire. Then circumstances would evolve to force me to ask the same questions directly and indirectly that centuries ago a young, helpless warrior had asked on the battlefield of Kurukshetra. Realisations and answers would emerge out of the experience and imbibing the learning, the process of translation would resume.

Around that time, my mother became terminally ill and amidst the pain, chaos, caring, and mental trauma, the Geeta stayed as a constant companion and diversion. Mother passed away in my presence and the chapter on death and the soul was imbibed through experience. Somewhere there, in the intensity of it all, I lost my connection...

Perhaps there was more to be learnt, from the subtle, subtler to the subtlest, as Meena ji so often states. Reading and chanting the Geeta at the time of passing is a ritual that is followed in our culture, since at such times being frail mentally, the seeds of its wisdom, are sown effortlessly. For almost six months hence, I did not even open this powerful source of detachment and solace. Then slowly as realisations dawned, sanity and direction returned, the Geeta came back to life, becoming an even greater source of strength.

The beauty of the Nitya Geeta is that its dialogues flow effortlessly as they crop up in the mind, pretty much as Arjun poses questions to the Supreme Being. The answers are clear, concise and applicable to every difficult situation. The war within is no different from the Mahabharat.

The Nitya Geeta descended in Meena ji when she was in absolute disarray and disillusioned by the worldly ways. In the moment of intense surrender, she heard a voice that instructed her to invoke Maa Saraswati. As she started to pen down all that came to her in intense dhyan, at a time not chosen by her, in the words not selected by her, the hands merely manifesting effortlessly, the gyan poured.

The Geeta mostly descended on Wednesdays, the time of manifestation meticulously noted. Through these trans-writings Meena ji played with words having merged with the divine essence, she felt divinity in everything. Her personal realisations aligned beautifully with the divine colloquy, adding a fresh perspective to the Geeta.

Nitya Geeta is unique because it is the purest, livable, practically applicable version of true spirituality that transcends religions. The Bhagwad Geeta is an outcome of living Veds and Upanishads. And the Nitya Geeta is the outcome of living the Bhagwad Geeta, making it a link in this process of evolution. Explanations of the Geeta may change over time, but the gyan it imparts remains the same. And something new has to be added to it according to the time and evolution of Consciousness.

The Nitya Geeta highlights how to relate to the Geeta in daily life. This can be explained only by the one who has immersed herself in the essence of the Geeta. Through her connection with Krishn Consciousness,

Meena ji realised that 'the Geeta is the Maha-mantra', supreme mantra for manav to become Maha-manav, human to become a superb human being.

Meena ji's contiguity with Consciousness and subsequent evolution, highlight the fact that any human being living a normal life, who neither belongs to a formal religious stream, nor is well-versed in scriptures and rituals, can merge with Supreme Consciousness by doing sadhna of living the wisdom of the Geeta. It is a guide for the ordinary to become extraordinary.

Meena ji says that whenever we have a question, the answer is already present, we only need to be open to it. The one in divine surrender, leading a life of truth love and karm will get answers in time.

Some English words are limited in their capacity to translate and express the depth and vastness of Devnagari. Hence, the closest words that convey the meaning have been used. The manuscript is compiled from Meena ji's handwritten diary, and in places, her musings are inserted in italics.

Guided by the Geeta, Pranam Movement, founded by Meena ji, is based on the four pillars of Truth Love Karm and Light — the Mana Marg, the path that cannot be negated.

Finally, with all humility I express my gratitude for this beautiful journey of life with Pranam under the ever-watchful intense eyes of Meena ji.

The Nitya Geeta is indeed the song of the soul, of the one purified by the penance of life and enlightened by Supreme Consciousness. It is a perpetual joy to be a witness to this manifestation at play in today's age. The Geeta has truly returned anew.

Hariom Tatt Satt

Anubhuti
August 15, 2017
Noida

P.S. This translation was completed on Janamashtmi, the descent of Shree Krishn. It may be an indication that, as often stated by Meena ji, now is not the time to delve into the leelas of his youth only but to live the greatest message offered by Shree Krishn — the Geeta.

|| ॐ ||

हरि ॐ तत्सत् फ्र ॐ फ्र   शनिवार
क्रीं प्रां प्रीं प्रौं सः शनैश्य नमः   28.6.2014   23

ह्रीं श्रीं क्लीं कृष्णाय गोविन्दाय
गोपी जन

क्लीं कृष्णाय नमः वल्लभाय स्वाहा

षट्कोण अग्निपुर अग्निपुर
षट कोण

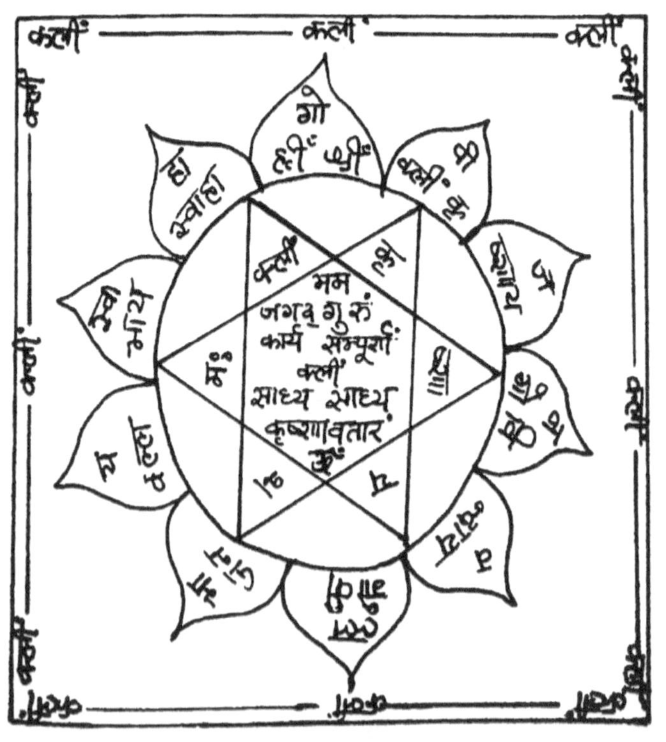

Meena Om is a modern-day seer-scientist, practical visionary, and a spiritual mentor. Through a spiritual movement called Pranam, she has been working relentlessly to spread the message of Truth; Love; Karm, right conduct at the right time; and Light, eradication of ignorance wherever prevalent.

Besides providing clear, tangible insights into true spirituality, Meena ji exemplifies how original Vedic seer-scientists functioned, manifesting supreme truths by maintaining perfect synchronicity with Nature and the Universal mechanism.

Meena ji's perceptions of Supreme Consciousness, expressed through trans-writing, are manifesting continuously in a flow and are being recorded in a spontaneous and sincere manner. Hidden in these writings is profound wisdom that imparts clarity and intense insights into real spirituality. The subtle and lyrical symmetry of Nature at its macro as well as micro levels is expressed and delivered with ease through her effortless connection with Nature. She even talks about an inner unseen anatomy that contains answers to many scientific conundrums yet to be explored by formal sciences.

Meena Om is a 'de-mystified' mystic, who aspires to ignite minds of genuine seekers to seek, get empowered to listen to the time call and act accordingly for the welfare of all, towards harmonious co-existence.